A SOCIABLE GOD

1 2 3 4 5 6 7 8 9 0 D O C D O C 8 7 6 5 4 3 2

ISBN 0-07-070185-7

Library of Congress Cataloging in Publishing Data

Wilber, Ken
A sociable God.
Bibliography: p.
Includes index.
1. Religion and sociology. 2. Psychology, Religious. I Title
BL60.W53 1983 306.6   82-15241
ISBN 0-07-070185-7   AACR2

DESIGN BY NANCY DALE MULDOON

A SOCIABLE GOD

A Brief Introduction to a
Transcendental Sociology

KEN WILBER

NEW PRESS

McGRAW-HILL BOOK COMPANY

New York St. Louis San Francisco
Hamburg London Mexico Toronto

CONTENTS

FOREWORD

OUR religions, our Gods, and our selves may not be quite
what we thought. That of course is nothing new. Indeed
history can be read as an expression of their progressive
evolution, as Ken Wilber has elegantly done in *Up from
Eden*. For religion has been the driving force behind a
vast range of behavior, calling forth the highest expressions of human nature and providing excuses for the
lowest. Whole cultures have lived, killed, and died for
their beliefs. Small wonder then that religion has been
one of the central interests of psychology, sociology, and
anthropology.

Throughout most of Western history religion was preeminent in defining our reality, and woe to the individual
who suggested other views or even other methods of
discovering truth (e.g., Galileo). Yet recent history, as if
in recompense, has not been kind to religion; it has steadily lost ground to science and rationalism as the major
purveyors of reality. Indeed, from the rational perspective, religion is frequently seen as a relic of prescientific
thinking, an unfortunate carryover from less sophisticated times. God, if not dead, is at least moribund,
surviving only through the unrequited longings of the
psychologically immature.

Yet in recent years God has been staging a dramatic
comeback, not only in traditional guise but in a full range
of diverse forms, Eastern and Western, exoteric and esoteric, fundamentalist and gnostic. Christianity has seen
both a fundamentalist revival and the reappearance of
contemplative-mystical approaches. In addition, there
has been an unprecedented influx of non-Western religions and disciplines—yoga, Zen, TM, and all. Some
of these differ so fundamentally from our traditional be-

liefs and practices as to call into question some of our most basic assumptions about the very nature of religion itself. Buddhism, for example, posits no supreme being or God and centers around a rigorous program of mental training explicitly aimed at controlled psychological processes and states of consciousness. On the morbid side, there is also no end of religious pathology; cults, Jonestown, and Moonies have become household terms.

Small wonder then that the study of religion, in any of its forms, has assumed new importance for both psychology and sociology. Sociologists have been particularly active in studying "the new religions" and in attempting to connect their emergence with larger social patterns and possible pathologies. They have therefore tended to link religious motivation to inadequacies at the social level, and immaturities at the psychological. And of course they are often correct since there is no shortage of evidence that religious immaturity and pathology reflect their psychological counterparts.

And yet the nagging question remains, Could we be missing something? Is this really all there is to religion? After all, the great saints and sages, Buddha, Christ, Lao Tzu, Shankara, Aurobindo, and others have been said to represent some of the highest levels of human development and to have had the greatest impact on human history. So at least said Toynbee, Tolstoy, Bergson, James, Schopenhauer, Nietzsche, and Maslow, among others. Thus we may ask, Are our guiding sociological assumptions, theories, and methodologies adequate to identify not just immaturity and pathology but also the heights of human experience and development that certain of the great religions claim are both possible and achievable through training?

It is the goal of this book to ensure that these heights are indeed identifiable, and it takes its psychological framework from recent developments in what has come to be known as transpersonal psychology.

The last two decades of psychological research have seen a dramatic surge of interest in areas such as the nature of consciousness and consciousness-modifying technologies, self-regulation of psychophysiological processes, and non-Western psychologies. The general trend has been toward the recognition that there exist states of consciousness, levels of psychological maturity, and degrees of voluntary control beyond those formerly thought to define the human potential. Humanistic psychology first emerged in an effort to focus attention on these areas; transpersonal psychology followed when even the humanistic model proved inadequate to encompass the full range of phenomena being studied. The term "transpersonal" was chosen to encompass those experiences and states in which the sense of awareness and identity apparently went beyond (*trans*) traditional personality and ego.

In the West they were commonly called peak experiences and were initially assumed to occur only rarely and involuntarily. However, certain Eastern psychologies and religious disciplines were subsequently found to contain not only detailed descriptions of such states but also instructions and technologies for attaining them at will. Suddenly, and with no small surprise to Western psychologists, it began to become apparent that the esoteric core of certain of the great religions, Eastern and Western, which had formerly seemed nonsensical or even pathological, could be understood as technologies for the voluntary control of psychological processes and consciousness. To take but one specific example, meditation could now be seen as an attentional training strategy rather than as a regressive and autistic escape from the world, and this new interpretation now has significant support from empirical research.

Thus it was not that the great religions were necessarily pathological but rather that, prior to an understanding of the nature of such phenomena as state dependency, our own Western psychological framework had not been readily able to encompass such phenomena.

Of course this is not to say that all things Eastern or religious are of this ilk. There are clearly distortions, dogma, pathology, misunderstanding, and misuse around all religions. Indeed, the pragmatic core of rigorous mental training is often buried under exoteric trappings and dogma, or else reserved as an esoteric core for the few deemed able to meet its exacting demands. But where this core of mental training is found, it tends to display marked similarities among apparently quite diverse systems and to point to common psychological principles, world views, and transcendental states: the so-called "transcendent unity of religions," "perennial philosophy," and "perennial psychology."

The addition of a transpersonal dimension to traditional psychological models has thus allowed the meaningful reinterpretation of a major sphere of human activity. However, sociological theory has tended to lack a corresponding dimension and has thus sometimes been susceptible to an overly reductionistic approach in its studies of religion. This book therefore aims at adding a transpersonal dimension to sociological theory.

No one is more qualified to do this than Ken Wilber, who is recognized as the preeminent theoretician of transpersonal psychology. In his numerous books and papers he has provided an unparalleled integration of the world's major psychological and religious systems. In *The Spectrum of Consciousness* he suggested that the apparent conflict between different psychological and religious systems could be resolved by seeing them as addressing different and partly complementary structures of consciousness and levels of the unconscious. In *The Atman Project* he suggested a model for developmental psychology that extended through not only childhood and adolescence but also the various levels of enlightenment. In *Up from Eden* he applied this model to human evolution at large.

Now in *A Sociable God* he takes this same model and uses it as a developmental framework against which the various levels of social interaction can be assessed. This therefore provides a corrective addition to current methods of sociological analysis such as phenomenological-hermeneutics that have lacked critical criteria for hierarchical evaluation. It also provides a means for avoiding the trap of taking one level of social interaction and making it paradigmatic for all. For example, Marx interpreted all behavior in terms of economics, and Freud in terms of sexuality. Art, philosophy, religion, and all "higher" activities thus became expressions of economic oppression or sexual repression.

To this developmental framework Wilber also adds an analysis of the various epistemological modes, the ways in which we obtain knowledge. The fact that sensory, intellectual, and contemplative modes yield different realms or categories of knowledge that are not wholly equivalent or reducible one to another is often forgotten. Conceptual symbolic knowledge cannot wholly be reduced to the objective sensory dimension, nor the contemplative to the conceptual, without resulting in what is called category error. Thus the method for establishing the validity of each realm's knowledge is specific: analytic-empirical for objective data, hermeneutics for symbolic communication, and direct gnostic apprehension for the contemplative.

After delineating these general schemata, Wilber then applies them to specific, especially religious, issues confronting sociology today. First he performs the much needed task of differentiating among the many and varied ways in which the term religion has been used, suggesting that much current confusion stems from imprecise or even mixed usage.

Next he turns to the evolution of religion and interprets its current status and directions against his developmental framework. Our current progression away from mythic belief toward increasing rationalization has been widely interpreted as evidence of an anti- or post-religious evolution. But Wilber reframes this whole movement by noting that this type of progression is an appropriate phase-specific shift as the pre-rational yields to the rational *on its way to the trans-rational*. From this evolutionary perspective our current phase is seen as anti-religious only if religion is equated, as it often is, with the pre-rational rather than with any of several levels on the pre-rational–rational–trans-rational developmental hierarchy. This remarkable perspective also allows a method of determining what Wilber calls the authenticity of a religion: the degree to which it fosters development to the trans-rational levels. This he differentiates from "legitimacy," which he defines as the degree to which a religion fills the psychological and social needs of a population at its current developmental level. And all this leads directly to one of the more seminal parts of the book.

The current religious ferments and the new religions can be examined precisely in light of their responses to the current developmental phase of increasing rationality. Wilber suggests that three major types of sociological responses are now occurring: first, attempting to cling to the now outmoded mythic levels (e.g., "moral majority"); second, embracing the ongoing rational-secularization process (such as the liberal intelligentsia tend to do); and third, in a minority of cases, attempting actual trans-rational transformation, not by denying rationality but by embracing it *and* going beyond it via intensive yogic-gnostic practice. It is this latter group that Wilber suggests may provide effective catalysts for a broader-scale evolutionary advance, if indeed such is to occur. The importance of such widespread maturation to full development of the rational level, and then beyond, is difficult to overestimate. Our willingness and ability to correct the vast amounts of worldwide suffering from preventable causes such as malnutrition, poverty, overpopulation, sociogenic pathology, and oppression, as well as to avoid massive, if not total, self-destruction, may depend on it. The importance of Ken Wilber's contribution of a testable, critical, comprehensive, sociological model capable of guiding assessments of these evolutionary shifts is likewise not to be underestimated.

This could have been a very lengthy book. The number of novel ideas and suggested syntheses it contains within its few pages is remarkable. The author has chosen to give us an heuristic framework rather than a detailed text. Nonetheless, this outline may well be sufficient to keep both sociologists and psychologists busy researching and filling it out for many years to come, for it has suggested a way to move the psychology and sociology of religion to a new watershed.

ROGER WALSH, M.D., PH.D.

PROLOGUE

THIS book is an introductory overview of the psychology and sociology of religion, with particular emphasis on how modern sociological theory might benefit from a dialogue with the perennial philosophy—that is, from transcendental or "transpersonal" perspectives (hence the subtitle). In the terms of current sociology, it is an introduction to a "non-reductionistic" sociology of religion (or world views in general), and it is based on various tenets taken from modern functionalism (e.g., Parsons), hermeneutics (e.g., Gadamer), and developmental-structuralism (e.g., Habermas), all of which are carefully set in a context of transcendental or transpersonal possibilities (e.g., William James). The book is not "merely metaphysical" or "hopelessly idealistic," however, for it contains concrete methodologies and strategies for hypothesis formation and testing.

Of course, a transcendental or transpersonal sociology is, in part, a new type of approach; nonetheless, its topic is of direct and immediate relevance to any number of current social, psychological, and religious theories and topics, including the new religious movements in America, cults, the influx of Eastern mystical traditions, the breakdown of "civil religion," the psychology of religious experience, meditation, the process of sociological "legitimation" of world views, humanistic and transpersonal psychology, moral development, and so on—all of which, more or less, are woven together in the following pages by virtue of the scope of the topic itself. Scholars as well as educated laypersons concerned with

1   any of those topics might thus find the book of interest.

I have, then, tried to provide the briefest possible statement of, and introduction to, a general transcendental sociology. *Brief*, for several reasons. For one, this is, in part, and as far as I know, the first attempt to broach the transcendental aspects of the subject, and first attempts deserve brevity. For another, I wished this book to be a concise statement of the *possibilities* of this field and not a rambling dissertation on its necessary content. The book itself, although scholarly, is meant to be accessible to the educated layperson interested in psychology, sociology, and religion, and brevity makes it that much more accessible. For scholars in these fields, my presentation of "just the skeleton" will allow them to add the meat and flesh of their own ideas, perspectives, and insights, without any further interference from me, thus arriving at a variety of fleshed-out products by virtue of their own additions (coproductions, as it were). I believe this skeleton is sound enough, and new enough, that no more need be presented in this initial outing; to do so would simply run the risk of overdetermining a new and fragile topic. Finally, by keeping the account sparse, I felt that the volume might more easily be used as an auxiliary text or for outside reading in any number of college or graduate courses on closely related topics.

But because this *is* a short introductory presentation, I have occasionally had to state my suggestions in a rather dogmatic and conclusive fashion. I would therefore like to emphasize that the following suggestions are, in fact, offered as hypotheses, and hypotheses that can potentially be tested—and potentially rejected—by a set of experimental methodologies. These methodologies are outlined in the last chapter. I might also say that this is one of those slightly awkward topics whose individual parts can better be understood once the overall topic is itself grasped, and thus this is one of those books that benefit from a second reading. At the least, the reader might, at the end, briefly reflect on the points that went before and see if they do not make a type of comprehensive sense perhaps not obvious at the first reading.

The word "transpersonal" might be new to some readers. For the moment, suffice it to say that it involves, in part, a sustained and experimental *inquiry* into spiritual, or transcendental (transpersonal), or "perennial philosophical" concerns. And it does so *not* in order to uncritically validate all so-called "religious experiences" but to attempt to develop legitimate and reproducible means for differentiating between authentic spiritual experience, if such indeed exists, and merely psychotic, hallucinatory, grandiose-exhibitionistic, paranoid, delusional, or other abnormal or pathological states. It is a *critical* discipline.

But because this book is, in part, one of the first attempts to bring a transpersonal or critical-transcendental dimension to sociology, it is faced with both a blessing and a curse. Blessing, in that one may, with only a modicum of intelligence, make pioneering observations, by simple definition. Curse, in that there are no precedents against which to judge the real value of those observations. This is quite different from even the recently introduced field of transpersonal psychology, for transpersonal psychology—under different names—actually goes all the way back to Plato, Augustine, and Plotinus, in the West, and Buddhaghosa, Patanjali, and Asanga in the East, and it can claim such contributors as Kant, Hegel, Bradley, Eckhart, C. G. Jung, William James, Jaspers, *et al.* This is because psychology itself, as a distinct discipline, goes back at least to Aristotle's *De Anima*, and transpersonal psychology, by whatever name, is simply the approach to psychology from the perspectives of the *philosophia perennis,* an approach that is thus as old as the perennial philosophy itself. Under the title "transpersonal psychology" it is, in a sense, a new and modern discipline, but it has a very old

3   and very honorable history.

Sociology, on the other hand, is counted as perhaps the youngest of all the human sciences. Certain Renaissance and Enlightenment scholars—Hobbes, Locke, Rousseau, Machiavelli, Montesquieu, Vico—were sociologists of a sort. But it was not really until the nineteenth century, when the concept of *society* was finally distinguished from that of the *state,* that sociology emerged as a distinct discipline. The term "sociology" itself was not coined until 1838, by Auguste Comte, and its two great "founders," Émile Durkheim and Max Weber, wrote their first pioneering works in 1893 and 1920, respectively. A mere few decades ago.

Here is the catch: sociology, yet an infant, arose in an intellectual climate largely dominated by the then-fashionable scientific materialism, and many of its early proponents were overly influenced by mechanistic science (e.g., Comte) or material interactions (e.g., Marx), with the result that their sociologies are expressly reductionistic. Even that sensitive scholar Durkheim has recently been labeled, by Robert Bellah, as one of the two "great reductionists" in human sciences (the other being Freud). Being such a young science, sociology has only recently moved to correct these reductionistic trends, by, among other things, using models based on living and not mechanical systems (e.g., Parsonian functionalism) and introducing phenomenology and interpretive disciplines, or the study of the *meaning* of mental acts *as* mental acts and not merely as reducible to empirical-objective behaviorisms (Schutz, Berger, etc.).

All of that is good news, and all of that will be touched upon in the following pages. Beyond that, however, sociology has still not been opened to those concerns embodied in the perennial philosophy. On the one hand, this is because sociology is indeed an infant; it had not the advantage of being exposed to a Plato, a Spinoza, a Hegel, a Leibniz—all perennial philosophers of a sort.

4 On the other hand, it is only recently that a modern,

experimental, and systematic inquiry into the essential tenets of the *philosophia perennis* has been undertaken (largely by transpersonal psychologists), and so, prior to this, just exactly how to infuse sociology with genuinely transcendental or transpersonal concerns might not have been all that apparent anyway. In any event, I believe the time is now ripe for such an infusion.

The point is that the modern psychology of religion ought to have something to offer the modern sociology of religion, and this book is a short introduction to both.

1

THE BACKGROUND PROBLEM VIS-À-VIS RELIGION

THE aim of this book is to suggest some contributions that transpersonal psychology might be able to make to the science of sociology, and especially the sociology of religion, by first, sketching out the basics of transpersonal psychology, and second, transposing these basics into the categories and dimensions of modern sociological theory. That done, specific topics and problems—such as the new religions, cognitive validity of religious knowledge, some definitions of religion itself, hermeneutics and structuralism in religious universals, methodology of religious inquiry, and so forth—will be broached. It should be emphasized, however, that because of the large amount of theoretical ground that has to be covered quickly, this presentation will necessarily take place on a very tentative, generalized, and informal level.

The initial problem, for both the psychology and sociology of religion, is to provide theories and methodologies for determining or understanding the purpose, and perhaps secondarily the validity, of religious involvement. I would like very briefly to review the major sociological (and orthodox psychological) responses to this problem, in order to highlight the areas to which transpersonal psychology might eventually contribute.

A. *Primitivization Theory*

One of the first and apparently reflex approaches is "primitivization," which views religion in general as the product of lower or primitive stages of human development or evolution. In sociology, for example, Comte's famous "law of three" sees historical evolution as moving from myth-religion to metaphysics to rational science, in which case religion is simply viewed as a primitive consolation for a primitive mentality. Transposed by modern developmental psychologists, this phylogenetic development seems to find many parallels in today's ontogenetic development: the infant goes from prototaxic magical thinking to parataxic mythical thinking to syntaxic rationality.[87] Religion, it again seems, is prompted by fixations or regressions to infantile magic or childish myth, the latter being particularly marked by Oedipal object-relations and thus susceptible to paternal or especially patriarchal introjections and subsequent projections as a heavenly Father,[29] now loving, now vengeful, now jealous, now forgiving—everything you ever wanted to know about Jehovah. From primitivization sociology to rational-emotive theory to psychoanalysis to orthodox cognitive psychology, this "religious = childish" formalization has been pandemic, with Freud himself *(The Future of an Illusion)* leading the way.[31] Piaget himself has extensively traced out the magical, mythical, "religious-type" thinking of early childhood and documented how such thinking tends to drop out as more formal and rational modes of thought emerge and develop.[70]

Now that particular developmental sequence—magic to myth to rationality—is not to be denied, as we will soon see in detail; problematic is its capacity to explain all, or even most, of the essential contours of religion. To give only the mildest objection now: even if all religious involvements were indicative of infantile-childish cognitions, that would at best explain their source but not

8

their function or purpose—their *meaning* for those sub-
scribing to them and their function in society at large.

B. Functionalism

It is not uncommon, then, that if a sensitive scholar first
embraces primitivization as explanatory, he or she eventually moves on to some sort of functionalist approach
(e.g., Parsons, Merton, Luhmann), if not to completely
replace primitivization, then at least to supplement
it.[62, 69] In functionalism or general systems theory,
groups or societies are viewed as organic systems, with
each of their "parts" (religion, education, customs, etc.)
serving some type of potentially useful or necessary function. Religious symbolism is thus analyzed in terms of the
salutary functions it serves in such specific areas as pattern maintenance, tension reduction, goal attainment, and
so forth of the overall social organism. From this view,
religious symbolism, if indeed it functions adequately
(i.e., if it helps the system to reproduce itself), is to that
extent *appropriate*.

In general functionalism, the functions and meanings
of group or social activities are often divided into two
dimensions, manifest and latent. The manifest function
has a recognized value—it is more or less conscious,
explicit, and expressed. The latent function, on the other
hand, is neither recognized nor consciously intended—it
is more or less implicit and unexpressed. Merton,[62] who
introduced this distinction in sociology (cf. Freud's similar distinction in dreams), used the Hopi rain dance as an
example. The manifest function of the ritual is to bring
rain. However, such rituals also "fulfill the latent function of reinforcing the group identity by providing a peri-
odic occasion on which the scattered members of a group
assemble to engage in a common activity." The manifest
meaning is apparent to the members of the group; the
latent meaning, however, can usually be discovered only
by specific functional analysis, that is, by the attempt to
determine what the empirical and *objective* function of a

9

particular relationship actually is and does, despite what the subscribers say or think it does (the manifest and subjective explanation).

When it comes to religion, then, various rites, symbols, and beliefs can be seen as serving legitimate functions. For even if, on a manifest level, the religious symbols are not objectively "true" (e.g., even if the rain dance does not actually bring rain), nonetheless on a latent level the rites and symbols serve a very necessary, useful, and to that extent "true" function: they help preserve and protect the overall integrity and cohesion of the group (they help the system to reproduce itself). Thus religious symbols, whether or not "objectively true," can nonetheless serve a legitimate purpose in the self-regulating social system. In short, religion serves some sort of function, perhaps hidden, and therefore has some sort of meaning, perhaps latent, in a given group or culture.

This, of course, is very similar to aspects of pragmatic psychology, such as that proposed by William James. Religious symbols can be appropriate units in the functioning of the psyche, regardless of the "objective truth value" of their supposed referents. For James, the very *belief* in spiritual realities could serve a salutary purpose that itself validated—indeed constituted—the truth-claim of the belief.[51]

There is clearly merit to this approach, and we will want to retain aspects of it in our overall formulation (even as we will find a place for a type of limited primitivization). But the functionalist approach in and by itself is expressly reductionistic. Religion is not actually a communion with some sort of true divinity, spirit, or godhead; it is really not much more than a safety-valve function. Its referent is not actual divinity; its *referent* is merely other symbols in a circle of social transactions. In other words, religion is not really religious; it is not about very God, but about various god-symbols, them-

10

selves composed of merely human social reciprocities.

If used exclusively, this approach heavy-handedly negates or at least re-interprets the actual validity claims of the subscribers themselves, and thus bypasses or reduces the central part, the subjective part, of the phenomena it is asked to explain. Not surprisingly, it is forced to place the "real meaning" of religiousness exclusively in a latent dimension where it can hide from the objections of the subscribers. This is not to deny that there *are* latent dimensions and functions in a belief system, for there are; it is to object to the pandemic reduction of the manifest-subjective intentionality to a latent-empirical function.

Thus, for functionalism, Lao Tzu, Buddha, Krishna, and Christ were not really intuiting a transcendent ground of being, which is what *they* said they were doing (their manifest intent). The functionalist can find no objective evidence, no empirical referent, for this "transcendental ground," and therefore what these sages were *really* doing was serving some sort of merely latent function unknown to them. The transcendental ground, *as* transcendental ground, never enters the picture, contrary to everything the sages themselves actually had to say on the subject.

But there are orthodox objections to exclusive functionalist systems theory as well. Preeminent among them is the apparent fact that human goal states and values cannot be determined via empirical-analytic or merely objective methods.[32] For, unlike the merely biological systems that form the basis of the functionalist model, human interactions also possess conscious meanings, values, goals, and purposes, and these relations are not so much objective as they are intersubjective. Consequently, they are disclosed not so much by objective measurement and analysis as by intersubjective communication and interpretation, and these intersubjective interpretations slide through the system without leaving completely empirical-objective footprints.[38] For exam-

11

ple, one cannot easily devise an empirical-scientific test that will disclose the meaning of *Hamlet*. *Hamlet* is a mental and symbolic production whose meanings and values disclose themselves only in a community of inter-subjective interpreters. Functionalism, in its attempt to be empirical and objective, simply misses the essence of these intersubjective meanings and values. On the other hand, if one attempts to overcome this shortcoming by simply stipulating the goal values and states that will then guide analysis of the system, that amounts to a normative and interpretive as opposed to empirical approach, which functionalism claims to be. Trying to account for these normative-interpretive dimensions by feeding them back into the empirical functions of the system (e.g., Luh-mann) is again to reduce the former to the latter.

C. Phenomenological-Hermeneutics

As theorist-researchers begin to question this reduc-tionism (in its psychological or sociological forms), it is not uncommon for them to move from exclusively functionalist analyses to something resembling phe-nomenological-hermeneutics: from at least one com-pletely valid perspective, *the religious symbol is exactly what it says it is*. It is not merely a manifest function hiding the real latent function, or just a safety valve, or only a tension-reduction or social-cohesion mechanism—it is fundamentally what it says it is. If Buddha or Krishna was lucid and legitimate in his communicative meaning, and he said he was contacting a fundamental ground of being, then that is our only starting point. And if I want to *understand* that point, if I want to understand anyone else's symbols and meanings, then the best approach is some sort of *empathetic interpretation* (just as if I wished to understand *Hamlet* or any other symbolic commu-nication). I must *reproduce* in *my* awareness via *inter-pretation* the *inner* world or meaning of Krishna or Hamlet or Job or whomever, there only to grasp its essential message.[32,49,67,68]

The science of such interpretation is generally called "hermeneutics," from the Greek *hermeneutikos*, to translate or interpret, and from Hermes, god of science, commerce, and eloquence. Hermeneutics has its modern roots in general phenomenology, or the attempt to discover the nature and meaning of mental acts *as* mental acts, and not merely as reduced to various objective, sensory, and empirical displays. For a merely sensory-empirical object— say a rock—does not necessarily point to or refer to anything other than itself. But a *mental* event—a concept or symbol—by its very nature points to or *refers to* other entities and events, including *other* symbols, which themselves can refer to yet other symbols, and so on in an *intersubjective* circle of symbolic meanings and values. In short, a mental act *as* mental act is what Husserl called *intentional:* it has *meaning* or *value* because it refers to or embraces other occasions, including other meanings and symbols and values. Phenomenology is an attempt to directly study this realm of intersubjective *intelligibilia*, not merely the realm of objective *sensibilia*. And hermeneutics is simply the branch of phenomenology that is especially concerned with interpreting the meanings of these intersubjective or intentional symbols.

Accordingly, if I want to understand the meaning of a particular religious system, I must not do so in a merely empirical, objective, reductionistic fashion. I must first empathetically understand the system by reproducing or entering its intersubjective and interpretive circle (the "hermeneutic circle"). Schools differ as to whether interpretation should be empathetic or actually participant (where feasible), but some form of *inside understanding* and *interpretive engagement* is deemed absolutely fundamental. The *meaning* of a religious expression is not solely or even especially to be found in, for example, its

13   latent tension management, but rather in its manifest in-

tentionality and its intersubjective acknowledgment. And the way you—as an "outside investigator"—determine that intersubjective meaning is to enter (not necessarily physically) the hermeneutic circle itself, the circle constituted by the intersubjective exchange of linguistic symbols, an exchange that is always set in a particular *historical* context. Hence the common title: historical-hermeneutics. If I want to understand the religious meaning of the word "sin," for example, I must take into account the *historical* context of the symbol itself, because what is "sin" to one epoch is not necessarily "sin" to another (whatever happened to gluttony and sloth, once "deadly sins"?). Merely defining "sin" objectively misses its historical referents and thus leads to bad interpretations, bad hermeneutics, ethnocentric bias, and so forth.[33,34]

This general phenomenological-hermeneutical approach has had an immense influence on both the psychology of religion—James's *Varieties* is a type of forerunner—and the sociology of religion—Ricoeur, for example, or Robert Bellah's "symbolic realism," which is a type of hermeneutic Durkheim, if I am allowed to say that. Likewise, I have watched many psychologist colleagues move from an initial fascination with systems theory and psychocybernetics (the scurrying of information bits through personless neurons) to a more comprehensive system that also includes an attempt to grasp the *meaning* of that information in terms of a self that shapes and is shaped by history. The self as history, hopelessly interlocked with other selves as history, constitutes not merely information but a *story,* a *text,* with beginnings and middles and endings and ups and downs and outcomes, and the way you grasp the meaning of a text is via good interpretation: hermeneutics.

There is obviously much to be said for phenomenological-hermeneutics, and we will be drawing significantly on many of its tenets as we proceed. But

14

taken in and by itself, hermeneutics seems finally to suffer a series of unhappy limitations. Foremost among these is its radicalization of situational truth and its consequent lack of a universal or even quasi-universal critical dimension, a way to judge the actual validity, not just interpretive mesh, of a religious truth claim. Krishna may have been transcending, but was the Hopi really producing rain? How are we to differentiate the authentic from the less than authentic engagements? Hermeneutics of course denies that such a critical or universal dimension exists, thereby relativizing all cultural truths with the quite illogical exception of its own claim that such is always (i.e., universally) the case.

For hermeneutics, all religious expressions—indeed, all symbolic productions—are to be understood from the inside; *verstehenden* sociology at its extreme. If you are *in* the hermeneutic circle, consensual interpretive agreement is validation; if you are outside the circle, you are not allowed a judgment. In neither case can the circle itself be shown to be wrong, or partially wrong, or even just *partial*. Such theoretical absolutizing of cultural relativity often translates itself, in the field, into exasperation,[3] an exasperation apparently due in some cases, not to incorrect methodological application, but to a more native pre-understanding that not *all* religious expressions are "true" and that some form of critical appraisal is mandatory.

Hermeneuticists and symbolic realists, of course, reply that this exasperation must be due to methodological or interpretive malfunction, because there is no *external standard* against which religious expressions could possibly be critically appraised, without, it is said, committing reductionism. Thus, any attempt to say other than what the particular hermeneutic circle itself says is, in a priori fashion, charged with reductionism, and thus hermeneutics, in and by itself, under the guise that it is being "non-reductionistic," tends all too rapidly to slide into the limp notion that "*all* religions are true," a stance that precludes any sort of sustained critical appraisal. Hermeneutics has no teeth.

D. Developmental Structuralism

Not only does exclusive hermeneutics deny those truths of functionalist systems theory that *are* partially true—for example, the possibility that there are latent functions performed by a text outside the knowledge of the text—it also overlooks the advances made in modern structural-developmental sciences, especially in the lines of Baldwin,[8] Piaget,[70] Werner,[95] Kohlberg,[54] and Loevinger.[57] For the seminal discovery of these disciplines is that psychological structures develop in a *hierarchic* fashion. Barring arrest, regression, or fixation, each stage of development includes, comprehends, or subsumes the basic elements of its predecessors but adds significant structures and functions not found in its predecessors.[100] The senior level includes the junior but *not vice versa,* and it is that "not vice versa" that constitutes and establishes a very real hierarchy. Each senior stage displays a greater degree of structuralization, differentiation-integration, organization, functional capacity, and so on through a dozen variables found to define, via a strict developmental-logic, the meaning of the word *higher*. Thus, developmental psychologists speak unabashedly about *higher stages* of cognition (Piaget), ego development (Loevinger), interpersonal relations (Selman), moralization (Kohlberg), and even *quality,* as the psychoanalyst Rapaport explains: "*Structures are hierarchically ordered.* This assumption is significant because it is the foundation for the psychoanalytic propositions concerning differentiation..., and because it implies that the *quality of a process depends upon the level of the structural hierarchy on which it takes place.*"[76]

16   Accepting for the moment that psychology is always

also social psychology, this overall hierarchization is extremely significant, because it apparently gives us— perhaps for the first time—a paradigm to *adjudicate the comparative degree of validity* of various psychosocial productions (including religious expressions). A similar approach has already been suggested by Habermas,[41] who wants to use, among other schemes, Kohlberg's stage-structures of moralization to adjudicate the developmental level of interactive competence evidenced in various individuals and, indeed, societies and historical epochs at large.

Before looking more carefully at this hierarchic paradigm, let us note that Habermas explicitly recognizes it as a corrective to historical-hermeneutic inquiry. Habermas utilizes some of the essentials of hermeneutics, such as its emphasis on narrative history and communicative competence, but he stresses that against hermeneutics, as a *narrative foil,* must be placed the hierarchic realizations of a developmental-logic. The fact of *levels* of narrative development *imposes* on any given narrative a competency status that is not and cannot be determined solely by empathetic interpretation of the narrative itself. There is, in other words, some sort of *external corrective* to the hermeneutic circle, and that external corrective is a scheme of developmental levels of narrative competence.

Finally, we note that, by virtue of hierarchy, each higher structure of consciousness is potentially capable of *legitimately criticizing* the partiality, but not the phase-specific appropriateness, of its lower predecessors, precisely as, for example, a person of formal operational thinking can criticize the lopsided egocentrism of preoperational thinking, or a stage-5 moral stance will criticize the lack of perspectivism of stage-2 stance. In other words, structural-developmentalism seems to give us that universal or quasi-universal critical dimension or external corrective apparently lacking in merely hermeneutic, phenomenological, or symbolic realist approaches.

17

E. Our Overall Approach

With all of the above as background, we can now state that the crux of this book is the suggestion that there exists a hierarchy not only of psychosocial development but also of authentic religious development, and that, in fact, these two run precisely into each other as two ends of a single spectrum, and that, finally, the hierarchical nature of this spectrum will give us a critical-normative sociology of religion, one that is capable of *structurally analyzing* various religious expressions, assigning them a spot in the hierarchy, consequently adjudicating their degree of authenticity, and accordingly pronouncing that, in terms of an *overall critical sociological theory,* this or that religious engagement is *higher* than this or that other religious engagement, *precisely* as we now say, for example, a stage-6 moral response is higher than a stage-4 response. In addition to this developmental-structuralism, we will also find necessary, appropriate, but circumscribed roles for functional systems analyses, hermeneutical inquiries, and even a type of primitivization theory, attempting, as it were, to salvage the moments of truth of each of the approaches we have so briefly discussed.

Before we begin such a construction, we need some background information, particularly from the field of transpersonal developmental psychology.

2

THE HIERARCHY
OF STRUCTURAL
ORGANIZATION

A. The Orthodox Base

Here is a very simplified, streamlined, and composite version of the hierarchical levels of structural organization as discovered by orthodox developmental psychology (I have included a few of their Eastern psychological correlates for future reference).

1. *Physical:* the simple physical substratum of the organism (the first and lowest Buddhist *skandha;* the first and lowest yogic chakra; *annamayakosa* in Vedanta).

2. *Sensoriperceptual:* the areas of sensation (the second skandha) and perception (the third skandha) treated as one general realm; simple sensorimotor cognition (Piaget).

3. *Emotional-sexual:* the sheath of bioenergy, libido, élan vital, or prana (the fourth skandha in Buddhism, the *pranamayakosa* in Vedanta; second chakra).*

4. *Magical:* the beginning of the mental realms; this includes simple images, symbols, and the first rudi-

---

*For simplicity's sake, I will usually refer to these lowest three levels as "the" *archaic level.*

mentary concepts, or the first and lowest mental productions, which are "magical" in the sense that they display condensation, displacement, confusion of image and
object, "omnipotence of thought," animism, and so forth.
There is also a lack of perspectivism, or an inability to
clearly take the role of other. This is Freud's primary
process, Arieti's paleologic, Piaget's preoperational
thinking (the third chakra). It is correlated with Kohlberg's preconventional morality, Loevinger's impulsive
and self-protective stages, Maslow's safety needs, and so
forth.

5. *Mythic:* more advanced than magic, with a beginning of concrete operational thinking (Piaget) and a beginning of perspectivism (or communal role-taking), but
still incapable of the simplest hypothetico-deductive reasoning, consequently "mythic" in its operation (cf.
Gebser); the overall "lower mind" (the fourth chakra, the
beginning of *manomayakosa* in Vedanta and *man-
ovijnana* in Mahayana). It is correlated with Loevinger's
conformist and conscientious-conformist stages, Maslow's belongingness needs, Kohlberg's conventional morality, and so forth. Because of its overall *conformity*
status, we often refer to this general level as "mythic-
membership."

6. *Rational:* Piaget's formal operational thinking (the
fifth chakra, the culmination of manomayakosa and man-
ovijnana). It is the first structure that can not only think
about the world but think about thinking; hence, it is the
first structure that is clearly self-reflexive and intro-
spective, and it displays an advanced capacity for perspectivism. It is also the first structure capable of
hypothetico-deductive or propositional reasoning ("if a,
then b"), which allows it to apprehend higher or purely
noetic *relationships*. It is correlated with Loevinger's
conscientious and individualistic stages, Kohlberg's post-
conventional morality, Maslow's self-esteem needs, and
so forth.

Figure 1 indicates these general stage-structures and their hierarchical nature.

Figure 1

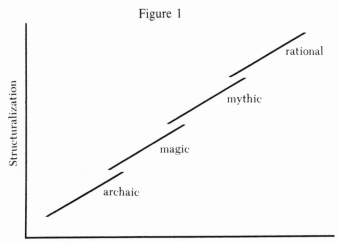

Temporal development

I have placed a gap between each structure to indicate that they are largely emergent or discontinuous in development; that is, they cannot be fully reduced to or explained solely in terms of their predecessor(s)—what has come to be called emergent evolution[71] or milestone development[57] (which does not preclude the continuous and linearly unbroken development *within* each level, or what is known as "polar development"). Each line in Figure 1 is evolution; each gap, revolution.

B. The Transpersonal Levels

The problem of this section is, Where in Figure 1 does religious expression belong?

Let us begin by noting that there is an increasing reacceptance, among developmental-structuralists, of the notion of phylogenetic/ontogenetic parallels: Primitive-paleolithic magic is similar in deep structure (*not* surface structure) to infantile–early childhood preoperational thinking; classic religio-mythic expressions are similar in deep structure to late childhood preoperational and beginning concrete operational thinking; and modern rational-science is top of the hierarchy with adolescent-to-adult formal operational and hypothetico-deductive reasoning.[5,66,95,105] As Arieti[5] explains,

> What is of fundamental importance is that the [two] processes to a large extent follow similar developmental plans. This does not mean literally that in the psyche . . . ontogeny recapitulates phylogeny, but that there are certain similarities in the . . . fields of development and that we are able to individualize schemes of highest forms of generality [deep structures, for example, as in Figure 1] which involve all levels of the psyche in its [different] types of development.

If we accept for the moment that there is some sort of truth to that idea—for I think there most definitely is—then we are faced with certain grave problems vis-à-vis legitimizing religious consciousness. For what we have, when Figure 1 is seen to be not only an ontogenetic but also a phylogenetic/ideogenetic chart, is actually a very sophisticated theory of religious primitivization, an update and slight expansion of Comte's law of three. For, if we treat religion as a structure among other structures, and not something potentially shared by them all (we will investigate that later), then *increasing historical development* clearly shows an eventually *decreasing religiosity*. Paleolithic humans had magic religion: totem ritual that expressed the confusion of human and animal ancestor, voodoo-like rituals, animistic beliefs, and so on. Neolithic and Bronze Age humans had classical mythic religion: gods and goddesses controlling their fate, with petitionary rituals and prayers offered by humans to their heavenly fathers and mothers. And then, finally, comes the revolution of rationality (starting with Greece *c.* sixth century B.C., reaching its stride with eighteenth-century Enlightenment thought but only today beginning to claim a clearly dominant structural role).[105] This increasing rationalization brought the eventual retreat of religion (in any conventional sense) as a widespread, legitimate world view, its place being taken increasingly by hypothetico-deductive reasoning, empirical-analytic inquiry, and technical interests, as sociologists from Weber onward have noted.

By this scheme there is no highly developed religious structure of consciousness, for the highest structure is rational-scientific. It appears that we have no choice but to capitulate to the primitivizationists, psychoanalysts, and such—religion is *basically* a primitive fixation/ regression to infantile magic or childhood myth (rationalized, if necessary). Such a *developmental argument, I* believe, can even disarm Bellah's refutation of psychoanalytic reductionism, because here the analyst is not interpreting religious symbolism in terms of something foreign to the person himself, but rather is demonstrating that the religious symbol has its own internal structure that *places itself* in the history of hierarchic structuralization of the person's psyche. Analysis merely helps the individual to remember and reconstruct this history so as to more clearly see how it is presently opaque in its influence. To say this is reductionistic is to say that helping a person move from stage-3 morality to stage 4, 5, or 6 is reductionistic.

There are only two ways out of this impasse. The first is to claim that phylogenetic/ideogenetic evolution is in fact devolution—that there actually existed in the past a historical Garden of Eden on earth, perhaps in the Bronze Age of mythic religion, and that we have gone steadily downhill since. Since evolution is really devolution, the *earlier* stages are really *higher*. To empirical scientists this might seem a somewhat silly notion, but I remind the reader that such sober and respected religious scholars as Joseph Campbell[23] and Huston Smith[86] have more than flirted with this idea. I have also found that among sympathetic scholars of religion it is something of a point of honor to believe this. Nonetheless, for various reasons it

is a concept I find thoroughly unconvincing, as only

someone could who entitled a book on the subject *Up
from Eden.*

The second way out of this impasse is to open the
possibility that there are stages of structuralization higher
than formal operational thinking. Ontogenetically, this
would mean that an individual today can develop beyond
exclusively rational forms of mentation to some sort of
higher stage or stages of consciousness as yet unspecified. Phylogenetically, it means that evolution is
still continuing and that human culture at large faces
further and higher levels of (r)evolutionary structuralization.

But that idea reminds us immediately of Hegel,[45] who
saw history as eventually transcending mental self-
consciousness in the absolute knowledge of spirit as
spirit. There are Aurobindo,[7] who maintained that evolution is driving toward supermind realization; Teilhard
de Chardin,[91] who saw it culminating in omega point, or
Christ consciousness at large; and the great Russian philosopher Berdyaev,[15] who concluded that evolution
moves from subconsciousness to self-consciousness to
superconsciousness (his words). Despite the excesses of
some of these presentations, the point is that the general
concept of evolution continuing beyond its present stage
into some legitimately trans-rational structures is not a
totally outrageous notion. Look at the course of evolution
to date: from amoebas to humans! Now what if that ratio,
amoeba-to-human, were applied to future evolution?
That is, amoebas are to humans as humans are to—what?
Is it ridiculous to suggest that the "what" might indeed be
omega, *geist,* supermind, spirit? That subconscious is to
self-conscious as self-conscious is to superconscious?
That prepersonal gives way to personal, which gives way
to transpersonal? That Brahman is not only the *ground* of
evolution but the *goal* as well?

What is specifically needed, however, beyond these
24 generalizations, is some sort of more precise specification

of what the higher structure-stages of consciousness might be. For various reasons, I first looked to the psychological systems of Hinduism and Buddhism for possible answers; I later found these answers echoed in Sufism, Kabalah, neo-Confucianism, mystical Christianity, and other esoteric traditions. What struck me about these traditional psychologies is that, although they often lacked the detailed sophistication of modern Western psychologies, they were perfectly aware of the general features of the level-structures so intensively investigated in the West (i.e., physical, sensorimotor, emotional-sexual, lower mental, and logic-rational). Nonetheless, they universally claimed that these levels by no means exhausted the spectrum of consciousness—there were, beyond the physical, emotional, and mental levels, higher levels of structural organization and integration.

For instance, Vedanta Hinduism claims there are six major structure-levels of consciousness.[26] The first and lowest is called *annamayakosa*, literally the level made of physical food, or the physical body. The second is *pranamayakosa*, the level of emotional-sexuality (prana is an almost exact equivalent of libido). The third is *manomayakosa*, the level of mind. This level also includes, besides rationality, the "dream aspects" of mentation; dreams, says Shankara, are basically wish-fulfillments, composed of the person's "fantasy and desires." The fourth is *vijnanamayakosa*, higher mental or transrational or intuitive cognition, the beginning of actual spiritual insight. The fifth is *anandamayakosa*, the level of ecstatic illumination-insight. The highest state is *turiya*, or Brahman-Atman itself, although it is not so much one level among other levels but the ground, reality, or suchness of all levels (*tathata*, the Buddhists call it).

Anyway, I undertook an explicitly hermeneutic reading of the world's great traditional psychologies, attempting to analyze and interpret the general structural units of meaning presented in the various classic texts. I practiced Zen Buddhism under various teachers for ten years, so I know at least one tradition "from the inside," via empathetic participation.

The result of this hermeneutical and practical encounter with the traditional psychologies was presented in *The Atman Project,* [101] although in an extremely skeletal fashion and without methodological explanation. The conclusion was that it is indeed plausible that there are higher stages of structural organization and integration, and that these higher stages increasingly display what can only be called a spiritual or transcendental tone. These higher structure-stages I called, largely after Vedanta, the psychic, the subtle, the causal, and the ultimate levels. If we add these higher stages to Figure 1, then we arrive at a tentative overall scheme of the developmental and structural spectrum of consciousness (see Figure 2; Brahman—or Dharmakaya or Kether or Godhead—is said to be both the limit-at-infinity of growth, which I have listed as the asymptote, and the ever-present ground of all levels of growth, which can be represented by the paper itself, which I have labeled "ground").

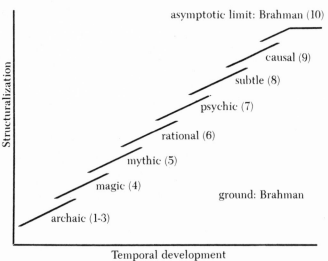

Figure 2

26

We can also draw this as a circle and then more easily add the three large domains of development— subconscious (prepersonal), self-conscious (personal), and superconscious (transpersonal)—although their precise alignments with the specific structures are, of course, somewhat arbitrary. (See Figure 3.)

Let me very briefly describe the higher or transpersonal levels, as disclosed in the various texts themselves. At the same time, I will correlate these levels with the basic types of *esoteric religious practice*, as suggested by such spiritual adepts as Aurobindo,[7] Free John,[22] and the Vajrayana tradition.[101]

The *psychic level* does not necessarily or even usually refer to paranormal events, although some texts say these can more readily or controllably occur here. More specifically, the psychic level can be best understood in reference to the level preceding it, that of formal operational or propositional reasoning, whose form is "if a, then b." The psychic level simply works with or operates on the results of formal mentation. That is, where the formal mind establishes higher relationships ("if a, *then* b"), psychic cognition establishes *networks* of those relationships. The point is to place each proposition alongside numerous others, so as to be able to see, or "to vision," how the truth or falsity of any one proposition would affect the truth or falsity of the others. Such panoramic or *vision-logic* (the technical term I use to describe the cognitive operations of this level) apprehends a mass network of ideas, how they influence each other, what their relationships are. It is thus the beginning of truly higher-order synthesizing capacity, of making connections, relating truths, coordinating ideas, integrating concepts. It culminates in what Aurobindo called the "higher mind." It "can freely express itself in single ideas, but its most characteristic movement is a mass ideation, a system or totality of truth-seeing at a single view; the relations of idea with idea, of truth with truth, self-seen in the integral whole."

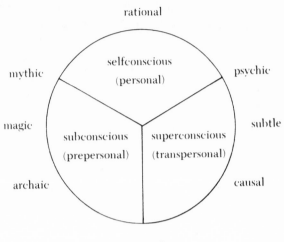

Figure 3

This is obviously a highly *integrative* structure. Although it might be thought of as the first and lowest of the transpersonal levels, it might also be described as the last and highest of the personal structures, beyond which lie more transcendental occasions. This highly integrated, highest personal structure is, in my opinion, precisely correlated with Loevinger's integrated and autonomous stages, Maslow's self-actualization needs, Broughton's integrated stage, and so forth. (In Eastern systems, this is the sixth chakra, the beginning of *manas* and *vijnamayakosa, tipareth,* etc.)

Many orthodox psychologists have already suggested that there are probably one or more cognitive stages beyond formal operational. Bruner, for instance, believes that some adults may progress from being intelligent (formal operational) to being intelligent about intelligence (or operating on formal operations). The structure we are proposing here—vision-logic—seems to fit that bill exactly, with the added advantage that it meshes explicitly with various Eastern systems (as expressly stated by, for example, Aurobindo, as the above quote makes clear).

Owing to the intense panoramic awareness offered at this level—or rather, at its most mature and highly developed state—the individual might begin to experience intense insight and even illumination, illumination that seems to go beyond thought into a type of vision, noetic, numinous, inspiring, often enstatic, occasionally ecstatic.[7,22] This can also result in a type of nature cosmic consciousness, or merging of self with the naturic universe (not to be confused with theistic or monistic mystical experiences, as we will see).[7] Those adepts mastering such states, via body manipulation and mental concentration, are generally known as *yogis*.

This does not mean that all who call themselves "yogis" actually attain this level. Nor does it mean that those who call themselves yogis never proceed higher than this level. It is just that the traditions that specifically describe themselves as *yogic* more often than not embody and express an understanding that most centrally reflects the psychic level, as clearly explained by Free John.[22] In the terms of chakra psychology, classic yogic discipline (hatha, kundalini, and ashtanga yoga) most centrally deals with those energies and insights leading from the first or root chakra, at the base of the spine, up through the sixth or ajna chakra, the "blue pearl," the "third eye," between and behind the brows. The ajna chakra is the embodiment of the psychic structure as here described. Beyond that point, consciousness leaves the psychic and enters the subtle.

The subtle level is said to be the seat of actual archetypes, of Platonic forms, of subtle sounds and audible illuminations (*nada, shabd*), of transcendent insight and absorption.[22,85,86,105] Some traditions, such as Hinduism and Gnostic Christianity, claim that, according to direct phenomenological apprehension, this level is the home of personal deity-form (ishtadeva, demiurge, yidam), cognized in a state known as *savikalpa samadhi* in Hinduism.[26,86,117] Overall, this is the level of the "illumined

mind" (Aurobindo); the culmination of manas and vijnamayakosa; a truly trans-rational structure (not pre-
rational and not anti-rational); intuition in its highest and
most sober sense (gnosis, jnana, prajna); not emo-
tionalism or merely bodily felt meaning or vegetative-
pranic-privitistic "hunch"; home of archangelic forms or
ideas; bijamantra, vasanas; beginning of seventh chakra
(the *sahasrara*); and, of course, the start of Maslow's
self-transcendence needs.

Those adepts who master these subtle realms of halos
of truth and light, revelations of subtle sound, and direct
soul-God-communion are generally known as *saints*.
Again, this does not mean that all who call themselves
saints have reached this level, nor that some authentic
saints do not surpass this level. It means only that the
disciplines, practices, and insights of the saintly traditions tend most centrally to reflect the subtle level of
structural organization. In the terms of shabd chakra psychology, the subtle region begins at the sixth or ajna
chakra, continues into the seventh or sahasrara, and then
discloses several more levels of subtler and subtler hierarchic structures secreted within and beyond the sahasrara
itself. Those adepts who master such subtle structures—
nicely symbolized (both East and West) by halos of light
at the crown of the head (sahasrara)—are generically
referred to as saints. Beyond these saintly revelations,
however, lies the causal/ultimate ground itself, or radical
and transcendental Consciousness as Such.

The *causal level* is said to be the unmanifest source or
transcendental ground of all the lesser structures, what
Aurobindo called the "overmind." It is realized in a state
of consciousness known variously as *nirvikalpa samadhi*
(Hinduism), *nirodh* (Theravada Buddhism), *jnana samadhi* (Vedanta), the eighth of the ten ox-herding pictures
(of Zen). This is the *anandamayakosa* (Vedanta), the
alayavijnana (Mahayana), *kether,* and so forth. Passing
fully through the state of cessation or unmanifest absorp-

tion, consciousness is said finally to re-awaken to its absolutely prior and eternal abode as spirit, radiant and all-pervading, one and many, only and all. This is classical *sahaj samadhi,* the state-condition of *turiya,* transcendental and unqualifiable consciousness as such, Aurobindo's "supermind," Zen's "One Mind," Brahman-Atman itself, the *Svabhavikakaya,* and such. Throughout this book I will, for convenience, treat the causal and ultimate "levels" as one—spirit in the highest sense, not as a Big Person but as the "Ground of Being" (Tillich), "Eternal Substance" (Spinoza), "Geist" (Hegel), the ground *and* the goal of development-revolution itself.

The causal/ultimate level does not involve any particular experience but rather the dissolution or transcendence of the experiencer himself, the death of the watcher principle. That is, the subject-object duality is radically transcended, so that the soul no longer contemplates Divinity, it becomes Divinity, a release the Sufi calls the Supreme Identity. If the subtle is the home of God and God-communion, the causal/ultimate is the home of Godhead and Godhead Identity.[7,22,26,81,86,101,117]

At that stage, asymptotic at infinity, one becomes radically egoless, or free of the separate self sense, thus assuming an absolute identity with all manifestation, high or low, sacred or profane. And yet, in being one with everything, only and all, there is nothing other to this state, and so it appears perfectly, radically, paradoxically, *ordinary*, as in the famous Zen saying, "How marvelous, how transcendental this! I draw water, I carry fuel." The adepts who realize this adaptation are generally known as *sages*.

As an example of the distinction between subtle saints and causal sages, we may take the Mosaic and Christic epiphanies.[105] The Mosaic revelation on Mt. Sinai has all the standard features of a subtle level apprehension: a numinous Other that is Light, Fire, Insight, and Sound (shabd). Nowhere, however, does Moses claim to be one with or identical with that Being. In India, at roughly the same time, a similar level of religious insight was expressed in the *Vedas*. Christ, on the other hand, does claim that "I and the Father are one," a perfect Atmic or causal level apprehension. In India, also at about the same time, a similar understanding was being set down in the *Upanishads,* where we find such causal/ultimate and Christic-equivalent statements as, "Thou art That," "This Atman is Brahman," "I am Brahman," and such, with the proviso that *anyone* can potentially attain this supreme identity, a tenet that was retained in Gnostic Christianity but lost/denied in exoteric-mythic Christianity, where Christ got "kicked upstairs," taking the supreme identity with him. Anyway, the difference between subtle saints and causal sages, or between the Mosaic-Vedic and Christic-Upanishadic revelations, is essentially the difference between savikalpa and nirvikalpa samadhi: in the former, one sees Being, in the latter, one becomes Being.

The point is that not only is there a variety of religious experience, there is a *hierarchy* of religious experience, with each successive stage—psychic, subtle, causal—being higher (by developmental, structural, and integrative standards) than its predecessor, and each correlative practice—yogic, saintly, and sagely—being likewise more ultimately revelatory.[105] This schema and its impact on the sociology of religion will be explored in Chapters 6 and 7. For the moment, let us simply note that this scheme enters decisively into the debate started by Zaehner and still raging among scholars of religion.

Zaehner[134] began by clearly and correctly pointing out that "what goes by the name of mysticism, so far from being an identical expression of the selfsame Universal Spirit, falls into three distinct categories," which are panenhenic or nature mysticism (e.g., Rimbaud, Wordsworth), monistic mysticism (e.g., Vedanta, Zen), and theistic mysticism (e.g., Christianity). Zaehner then used
this scheme in an attempt to give theistic mysticism a

higher status than panenhenic and monistic mysticism. Ninian Smart,[134] on the other hand, wants to champion the nondualist schools of religion (Vedanta, Mahayana, etc.) as being, if not higher, then at least not inferior, to theistic mysticism, and so consequently attempts to defuse Zaehner's position by denying the distinction between theistic and monistic mysticism, although he does accept the clear distinction between them and panenhenic mysticism.

To my mind, both are partially right. There *is* a distinction between panenhenic, theistic, and monistic mystical experience; they correspond almost precisely to the levels of structural organization we have termed psychic, subtle, and causal. But we turn the structural tables on Zaehner and side with Smart: theistic religion is not higher than monistic; in fact, the opposite: saintly communion with spirit is transcended by sagely identity with spirit. Thus, for example, when Watts[94] argues that monistic mysticism includes theistic mysticism, but not vice versa, he intuitively invokes the principle of hierarchization that adjudicates degrees of comprehensive validity.

Such, then, is one (simplified) version of an overall hierarchy of structural organization, one that includes prepersonal or subconscious components, personal or self-conscious components, and transpersonal or superconscious components. Whether or not that scheme is valid—indeed, the overall methodology of verifying (or rejecting) such schemes—will be explicitly dealt with in Chapter 9. In the meantime, we may *hypothetically* or provisionally accept it as valid. We will simply *assume* it is more or less the case and see if acting on this assumption helps clarify the psychology and sociology of religion. In the next two chapters, we will fill in a few more details of this overall model or hypothesis. Then, in Chapter 5, we will indeed begin acting on it.

3

THE COMPOUND INDIVIDUAL AS A LINK BETWEEN PSYCHOLOGY AND SOCIOLOGY

A. *Structures Are Structures* of *Relational Exchange*

What makes the above scheme—the ten or so levels of structural organization—not merely of relevance to sociology but somehow fused with sociology is the nature of each level itself. Namely, as *Up from Eden* tried to demonstrate, each level is a *process of exchange* with *corresponding* levels of structural organization in the world process at large, and that makes its psychology always also social psychology, as this chapter will now suggest.

For convenience' sake, I will reduce the number of levels of structural organization to five and use the names most familiar to Westerners: matter (1), body (2–3), mind (4–6), soul (7–8), and spirit (9–10). Now, since each of these levels of structural organization *transcends but includes* its predecessors, each structure of development enfolds, envelops, comprehends, or *compounds* the previous structures, much as the neocortex envelops the mammalian limbic system, which in turn envelops the reptilian stem.[100]

35

For this reason, and in an explicit attempt to connect developmental psychology and evolution theory with the philosophical groundwork of Whitehead[97] and Hartshorne,[44] we say that the human being is a *compound individual*—compounded of all the past levels of development and capped by the present level itself. Potentially, then, the human being is *compounded* of matter, prana, mind, soul, and spirit. The material body is exercised in labor with the physical-natural environment; the pranic (emotional) body is exercised in breath, sex, and feeling with other pranic bodies; the mind is exercised in linguistic communication with other minds; the soul, in psychic and subtle relationships; the spirit, in absolute relation to and as Godhead (or God-communion and God-identity). That is, *each level of the compound human individual is exercised in a complex system of ideally unobstructed relationships with the corresponding levels of structural organization in the world process at large.*[105]

Furthermore, humanity actually and literally reproduces itself on each level by an appropriate *exchange* of the elements of that level (with corresponding levels in the world at large). Humanity reproduces itself physically through the exchange of food secured by labor from the natural environment. It reproduces itself bodily (or biologically) via exchange of breath and sex. It reproduces itself mentally via education and communicative exchange. It reproduces itself spiritually (soul and spirit) via living exchange-transmission from adept to disciple.[105]

It thus appears that each level is intrinsically part of a sliding chain of relational exchanges and therefore *is itself* most fundamentally a *society* of exchanges, or social relationship. Even the material body, the very lowest level, is a *process* of food intake, assimilation, and release, and thus is always bound not to but as the community of its exchange partners. Sexual reproduction is obviously relational exchange. As for the mental level,

36

Lévi-Strauss (among many others) has clearly established that "In mathematics, in logic, or in life, a symbol must be exchanged with another person; in the act of exchange the symbol creates and maintains a relationship. Thus, the word *symbol* refers us back to the original Greek meaning: pact, bond, covenant, intercourse, or link."[107] And spiritual levels are not only exchanges with divinity, or communion-identity, but with divinity embodied as the spiritual master *and* the community of contemplative partners. Each level is a society of relationships or exchange occasions, with the human *compound* individual being a society of those societies, hopelessly interlocked with other humans in societies of *those*.[105]

The notion of relational exchange is sometimes expressed (redundantly) in the concept of "drives" or "needs." Since each level in the human being *is* a process of relational exchange with a corresponding environment, the human being has drives that express the need for those various environments: physical needs (food, water, air, shelter), emotional needs (feeling, touch-contact, sex), mental-egoic needs (interpersonal communication, reflexive self-esteem, meaning), spiritual needs (God-communion, depth), and so on. It is as if there were levels of "food" or "mana"—physical food, emotional food, mental food, spiritual food. Growth and development is simply the process of adapting to, and learning to digest, subtler and subtler levels of food, with each stage of growth marked by a phase-specific adaptation to a particular type of food. (We will return to the concept of phase-specific mana in the next chapter.)

The point is simply that, because each structure-level *is* a process of relational exchange (or food-needs), it is *necessarily* wedded to the objects that "satisfy" those needs. "Structure," "need," and "object-relations" are simply three aspects of the single exchange process that is each level. Take away the need-objects or food of the structure, and one takes away the structure itself. Take

37

away gross food, and the physical body begins to wither; take away vital food, feeling or warmth, and the emotional body begins to wither; take away "food for thought," intersubjective communication or symbolic exchange, and the mind begins to wither; take away transcendental food, spiritual relationship or grace-faith, and the soul begins to wither. In short, the notion of need or drive expresses nothing but the necessity for a structure to engage its corresponding object-relations or perish.

B. The Distortion of Relational Exchange

The developmental nature of these levels of structural organization and relational exchange (or food-needs) should be emphasized, however, because all of these levels are not *manifest* in individual humans from birth. Rather, the human individual apparently begins its growth and development by adjusting to the physical world (and its food), then to the emotional world (and its food), then the verbal-mental, then the transcendental, and so on (until growth stops in its own case). While these developments often parallel or overlap one another, nonetheless each level is built upon, and rests upon, the foundation afforded by its immediately junior level. However, and in my opinion this cannot be overemphasized, while the higher level "rests on" the lower, the higher is not caused by or constituted by the lower. The higher is in part *emergent*, discontinuous, milestone, revolutionary. The higher emerges *by way of* the lower; it comes *through* the lower, so to speak, but not *from* it, much as a baby chick comes through its egg shell but is not made of egg shells. For example, mind comes *through* libido, not *from* it. [105]

As the higher begins to emerge, it has to pass through the lower for the simple reason that the lower is *already* there, it already exists. As the higher appears on the scene, the scene *is* the lower or immediately junior dimension itself, and the higher is thus intially fused and confused with that lower—it is initially *undifferentiated* from it. Growth of the higher level is in part the process of vertical transcendence or *differentiation* from (and then integration of) the lower level through which it passed on its own emergence.[101] Thus, for example, prior to age 1½ or so, the infant cannot clearly differentiate the body-self from the physical environment; it lives in a state of protoplasmic indissociation (Piaget: "the self is here material, so to speak")[70]; bodyself and material world are largely undifferentiated. Between the ages of 1½ to 3 or so, the infant learns to differentiate the bodyself from the objective physical world, thus allowing the body to transcend that primitive-material fusion state.[50] As the symbolic mind begins to emerge (around 24 months or so), it is then initially undifferentiated from the body itself—mind and body are fused and confused (thinking is physiognomic, as Werner put it, or contaminated with sensorimotor categories, according to Piaget).[95,70] It is not until around age 7 or so that mind and body are first differentiated, and not until age 11–15 that they are clearly differentiated and mind finally transcends (but subsumes) the body itself.[57,70] Likewise, when (and if) the soul eventually emerges, it is initially fused and confused with the mind (it is clothed in mental forms and thoughts, not yet its own intrinsic visions and illuminations), and so on. The point is that in each case the higher emerges through, or by way of, the lower, only transcending the lower when it finally differentiates from it. This process of separation-individuation, or transcendence, marks each major stage of growth or emergence.[101] But we repeat: although the higher comes through the lower, it does not come *from* the lower, its essence being in part emergent.

Nonetheless, this emergence *through* the lower can have fateful consequences, because a distorted lower can *incline* the higher to subsequently reproduce the distortion on its own domain, much as a tough or brittle egg shell can damage the chick in its emergence. Perhaps a better metaphor here is a skyscraper: because the higher both comes through and then rests upon the foundation of the lower, a "tilt" in the first floor tends to cause a similar tilt in the second, and so on. Physical trauma can lead to emotional disturbances; emotional disturbances can generate mental instabilities, and so on.

But this is not an absolute causality; not only is the lower distortion only partially passed on, but *the higher level, by virtue of its emergent freedom, can often redress the imbalance.* We say, then, that a distortion in the lower *predisposes* (but does not cause) the higher to reproduce similar if dampened distortions in its own domain.

On the other side of the fence, the higher, because it does partially transcend the lower, can *repress* the lower. For example, sex cannot easily repress sex, but mind can repress sex, simply because mind is higher in structural organization than sex and can thus "come down on" sex.

Repression, as I use the term, is fundamentally an *internal* affair; it is instigated by the separate self in order to defend its own precarious sense of existence in the face of prior and always apprehended mortality. Repression is not caused by others or instigated by others, and it will occur, to various degrees, in even the most idyllic surroundings, simply because no setting is free of the skull that, as James said, will soon grin in at the banquet. Any aspect of the self-system—sensation, perception, emotion, cognition—that becomes too threatening, too laden with death-guilt, too charged with taboo, will be split from the system, outlawed, banished. Such repression does not actually destroy the "shadow," however, but merely sends it underground, where it registers its existence by sending up cryptic symbols (the hidden text) and disturbing symptoms.[101,105]

Although one individual cannot directly repress another, one individual can *oppress* another. This oppression has several consequences, two of which are (1) the oppression can disrupt and distort the exchange processes and capacities of any and all levels of the compound individual (as Marx found out for *material* exchange, Freud for *emotional-sexual* exchange, Socrates for *mental* communicative exchange, and Christ for *spiritual* exchange); and (2) the separate self, as it endures in (and attempts to adapt and adjust to) the atmosphere of such oppression, can and will *internalize* the originally external oppression, and internalized oppression then leads to *surplus repression,* repression over and above that which the self would induce on its own.[105]

Here are our generalizations so far: (1) the higher comes *through* the lower but not *from* the lower; (2) a distorted lower *inclines* the higher to reproduce similar distortions in its own sphere but (3) does not absolutely *cause* the higher to reproduce the distortions (the higher can to some degree dampen, reverse, amend, compensate, etc.); (4) the individual can defensively *repress* or internally distort, to one degree or another, any or all of his own levels of exchange (physical, emotional, mental, spiritual); (5) an external (powerful) other can *oppress* and distort an individual's levels of exchange; and (6) internalized oppression is surplus repression.

C. The Backbone of a Comprehensive Critical Theory in Sociology

I have elsewhere suggested how these generalizations can help us to reconstruct the essentials of such theorists as Marx and Freud without their reductionistic tendencies.[105] For, as we look at the levels of structural organization and relational exchange of the compound individual, it becomes obvious that many theorists have taken *one* level and tried to make it paradigmatic. If they take a higher level, as idealists do, they tend to elevate the lower levels to an exalted status they simply do not possess, or they tend to ignore the lower levels altogether.

41

Reading history according to Hegel, for instance, one always gets the impression that the material world might at any moment evaporate. This apparently annoyed Marx so much that he took the opposite but perfectly standard reductionistic approach: take a lower level, call it "the only really real" level, then reduce all higher levels to it, or at least explain all higher levels in terms of the lower. I need not tell you that Marx made the material level and its exchanges paradigmatic for *all* forms of existence. Freud did *exactly* the same thing for the next level up; emotional-sexual energies are *the* reality, and all else— culture, ego, mind, religion—is just a sneaky twisting of libido. At the next level up, we often find theorists who admirably refuse to reduce mental consciousness to sexual offsprings or material modes of production and, instead, accord mind its own rightful and higher place in development, but they tend to deny validity to realms higher than mind, realms that they then subject to standard reductionism—such "spiritual realities" are, at best, merely functional symbols without *real* referents. Communication becomes paradigmatic for such theorists (e.g., Habermas), and direct spiritual awareness is accorded something of a derivative status.

But you can see where such theorists *have* made absolutely crucial—if absolutely partial—contributions. Marx, for instance, compellingly demonstrated that when the material-economic exchange process is oppressed and distorted, then upon that distorted base tends to emerge alienated thoughts and feelings, or "false consciousness," and that the higher cultural productions of art, philosophy, and religion are thereby pressed as ideology into mere servants of oppression, each becoming, in its own way, an "opiate of the masses." Similarly, Freud demonstrated that emotional-sexual distortions tilted mental consciousness toward symptomatic sclerosis, blocked the free flow of mental ideas, and generally set up another

type of false consciousness in the form of a façade or

pseudo-self alienated from aspects of its own being (because it is alienated from aspects of relational exchanges
with others, hence the modern emphasis on object-relations theory).

Now we want to take all of those essentials with us, but
without their reductionism. For both Marx and Freud
went from saying, "A distorted lower predisposes the
higher to similar distortions" (correct), to saying, "The
distortions in the higher stem almost entirely from the
distortions in the lower" (incorrect; they stem partially
from them, but they can also be distorted for reasons
purely their own), to saying, "The higher itself must
therefore come from a distortion or frustration of the
lower" (even more incorrect; that amounts to making the
dynamics of repression/oppression paradigmatic for the
whole of development), to saying, "If there were no frustration of the lower, there would be *no* higher" (patently
absurd, but the reductionism is here completed). Hence
the orthodox Marxist position that when material exchanges are finally communalized, there will be *no need
for* philosophy, art, religion, and so forth; and the precisely correlative Freudian notion that without frustration
of instinctual urges, the mind would never emerge and
develop. Thus we utilize the valid insights of such theorists with the second generalization; we counteract their
reductionism with the first and third generalizations.

My point is that a comprehensive, unified, critical sociological theory might best be constructed around a detailed, multidisciplinary analysis of the developmental-
logic and hierarchic levels of relational (psychosocial)
exchanges that constitute the human compound individual. The theory would be *critical* in two important ways:
(1) adjudicative of each *higher* level of structural organization and critical of the comparative partiality of
each lower level, and (2) critical of the *distortions* in
exchange when and if they occur on any particular level.
43   The latter is a criticism *within* a level and demands as its

corrective a self-reflection on the historical formations that led to the distortion in the particular realm, economic, emotional, communicative, or spiritual. The former is a criticism *between* levels and demands as its corrective a *growth* to higher levels. The one is a horizontal emancipation, the other, a vertical emancipation. Neither can be dispensed with—growth to a higher level does not insure the healthy normalization of a lower level, and healing a lower level does not in and of itself produce a higher level. (We will return to this topic in Chapter 8.)

At a minimum, then, our levels of analysis would include (1) the physical level of material exchange, whose paradigm is food consumption and food extraction from the natural environment, whose sphere is that of manual (technic) labor, and whose archetypal analyst is Marx; (2) the emotional level of pranic (vital) exchange, whose paradigm is breath and sex, whose sphere is that of emotional intercourse, from feeling to sex to power, and whose archetypal analyst is Freud; (3) the mental level of symbolic exchange, whose paradigm is discourse (language), whose sphere is that of communication, and whose archetypal analyst is Socrates; (4) the psychic level of intuitive exchange, whose paradigm is siddhi (or psychic insight and vision-logic in general), whose sphere is yogic kundalini, and whose archetypal analyst is Patanjali; (5) the subtle level of God-Light exchange, whose paradigm is shabd-revelation and subtle illumination (savikalpa samadhi), whose sphere is saintly "heaven" (*Brahma-Loka*, the higher structural potentials of one's own compound individuality), and whose archetypal analyst is Moses/St. Paul/Kirpal Singh; and (6) the causal level of infinite exchange, whose paradigm is radical absorption in and as the Uncreate (nirvikalpa/sahaj samadhi), whose sphere is sagely Godhead, and whose archetypal analyst is Buddha/Krishna/Christ.[105]

44

4

TRANSLATION, TRANSFORMATION, TRANSCRIPTION

A. General Definitions

Before we finally apply this general theory to such specifics as the sociology of religion, new religions, cults, and such, we need a few technical definitions. If we simplistically think of the various levels of structural organization as so many floors in a tall building (in this case, ten stories, with the tenth being Brahman as highest level and asymptotic limit of growth, and the building itself being Brahman as the ground of all levels of growth), then (1) each floor itself is a *deep structure*, while (2) the variable components on each floor—its actual furniture, so to speak—are *surface structures;* (3) the movement of surface structures we call *translation;* (4) the movement of deep structures we call *transformation;* and (5) the relation between a deep structure and its surface structures we call *transcription.* Translation is moving furniture around on one floor; transformation is moving to a different floor; transcription is the relation of the furniture to each floor.

As a more accurate example, take a game such as checkers or chess. The surface structures are the various pieces and the various moves they make in a given game. 45 The deep structure is the *rules* of the game, the *patterns* that define the *internal relations* of the various pieces to each other. The rules holistically unite each piece to each other via patterned relations. The deep structure *defines the game*—you can alter the surface structures, make the pieces out of clay, plastic, or wood, and you still have the same basic game. You can even use rocks; all you have to do is transcribe the pieces according to the basic rules, that is, show how each piece fits into the rules of the deep structure. That relation of deep to surface structures is *transcription*. Finally, actually moving the pieces around on the board, or executing a play is *translation*.

Now if we change the deep structure, we change the basic rules of the game, and then obviously it is no longer the same game. We have *transformed* it into something else—perhaps another good game, perhaps a mess. Sometimes people will take checkers pieces and a checkerboard (if they do not want to buy a chess set) and transform them into chess by first changing the rules, or transforming the deep structure to that of chess; then transcribing the checkers according to their functions in chess, which means marking them as a rook, king, pawn, and so forth, and then finally translating these new surface structures according to the deep rules of chess.

Notice, even in this simple example, that the deep structures do not themselves change during the course of a game, nor are they influenced by the particular moves of a particular game. They are "a-historical." The surface structures do change, however, for each sequence of moves is different from game to game. What determines the particular course of moves is the sum of previous moves in the game so far. That is, the next move I make in a particular game will occur *within* the rules of the deep structure, but it is determined specifically by all the preceding moves (plus my present judgment about those previous moves). Those surface structures, in other words, are *historically conditioned*—not totally caused, but definitely molded to some degree, by past surface structures.

That is a small example of an overall postulate that refers to the basic levels of structural organization themselves: insofar as they have emerged, the deep structures of consciousness (e.g., as presented in Figure 2) are relatively a-historical, collective, invariant, and cross-cultural, whereas their surface structures are everywhere variable, historically conditioned, and culturally molded.[105] Thus, for example, the deep structure of the formal operational mind is, as far as we know, identical wherever it emerges, but the actual surface forms of that mind—its particular belief systems, ideologies, languages, customs, and so forth—are everywhere different, molded largely by the culture in which that mind itself develops.[70] This postulate (or rather, experimental conclusion) is similar to Chomsky's universal-grammar/specific-cultural-semantics,[24] except that it is not confined to the mental/linguistic levels but refers to all levels of basic structural organization (e.g., the deep structure of the physical body is everywhere identical— 208 bones, 2 kidneys, 4 limbs, 1 heart, etc.—but the surface activities of that body—the acceptable forms of play, work, sports, etc.—differ from culture to culture; and so on with emotional, subtle, causal, and other levels of structural organization). The idea itself took its initial impetus from Jung's work on archetypes as "forms devoid of content"[53] (although see Wilber[102]), but was bolstered by the cross-cultural investigations related to the work of Piaget, Kohlberg, Werner, and others. That this conclusion also and expressly applies to the deep and surface structures of the three stages of religious-mystical experience (psychic, subtle, causal) should especially be noted, for we will be drawing on this point in Chapter 7.

B. The Function of Translation: Mana and Taboo

Development or growth, then, seems to occur in two primary dimensions: horizontal-evolutionary-historical and vertical-revolutionary-transcendental, or, in short,

47

translative and transformative. Horizontal or translative growth is a process of transcribing, filling in, or "fleshing out" the surface structures of a given level; that is, assuming responsibility for the relational exchange of surface structures that constitutes the very lifeline or "food" of that level, a process that must occur if that level and the society of its reciprocal exchange partners are to reproduce themselves both moment to moment (or individually) and generation to generation (or collectively). Transformation, on the other hand, is a vertical shift, a revolutionary reorganization of past elements and emergence of new ones. It is synonymous with *transcendence,* although notice that transcendence is then not confined to the upper levels of consciousness (although it occurs there royally), but rather refers to the fact that *each* successive level transcends or goes beyond its predecessor(s): myth transcends magic, reason transcends myth, soul transcends reason, spirit transcends soul.[101]

Translation apparently has one major function: to integrate, stabilize, and equilibrate its given level; transformation apparently has one major function: to go beyond its given level. This dialectic of tensions seems to constitute much of the dynamic of development.[95,102] In this section, we key on its translative dimension.

Translation's major function—to integrate, stabilize, and equilibrate its given level—seems to have two basic facets, which we call *mana* and *taboo.*[105] Mana refers to the "food" of each level: for example, physical food, emotional food (love, belongingness), mental food (symbol, truth), spiritual food (illumination, insight). Translation is involved in securing the mana-food of its particular level via, of course, the processes of relational exchange (reception, assimilation, and release), for mana-food is exactly what *is* exchanged in those processes. Further, it seems that mana-translation, by virtue of this *necessary* relationship in and as a society of exchange partners, establishes and constitutes, in all of its phase-specific forms, the "glue" that binds the particular society in which the exchanges occur. With that in mind, and on any given level, we define "good mana" as that which is integrative, healthy, legitimate, and intrinsically binding, both within the boundaries of the particular individual and between the boundaries of individuals in the exchange process at large. "Bad mana," conversely, is less integrative or even disintegrative for the particular level.

We also suggest that, besides good and bad mana within a level, there are higher and lower forms of mana between levels. That is, each progressively higher level of structural organization seems to have access to a progressively higher mana, or higher truth-food. This does not, however, deny the relative and *phase-specific validity* of the lower truths. Nor does it, in and by itself, guarantee integrative stability for the higher level, since the bad mana of a higher level is often less integrative than the good mana of a lower one. But the potential for higher truth and integration is most definitely present, and so on balance we say that, for example, science is more truthful than myth just as saintly illumination is truer than science, but all serve their necessary and phase-specific functions and deliver themselves of appropriate-enough truths. Vertical growth is a series of phase-specific adaptations to increasingly higher levels of food, mana, truth, while horizontal growth is a process of learning to digest (intake, assimilation, release) that food on its own level.

For the taboo facet of translation, I have explicitly tied my arguments into those of Rank,[74] Becker,[10] and Brown,[19] although again I have tried to avoid what I feel are reductionistic elements in their theories. Their position is basically existential; it deals with the impact of death-apprehension on the individual psyche and the resultant attempts to deal with, or deny, the terror of

mortality.

For *death*, they maintain, is *the* fundamental taboo, the fundamental terror, and to the extent the separate self awakens to its own existence, then to that extent terror-angst is *inherent* in the self. ("The essential, basic arch-anxiety is innate to all isolated, individual forms of human existence. In the basic anxiety human existence is afraid *of* as well as anxious *about* its 'being-in-the-world.' ") Thus, there is simply but absolutely no way to avoid that terror except by repression or some other defensive or compensatory mechanism. Angst is not something the self suffers; it is something the self *is*.

Now the traditional psychologies—Hinduism and Buddhism, for example—agree perfectly and explicitly with that assessment (Buddha is regarded by many scholars, myself included, as having given *the* existential statement and analysis of the human predicament: *anicca, anatta, dukkha*—fleeting, selfless, pain). Wherever there is self, there is trembling; wherever there is other, there is fear. However—and this is where the traditions transcend mere existentialism—these psychologies maintain that one can go beyond fear and trembling by going beyond self and other; that is, by transcending subject and object in satori, moksha, the supreme identity.

But those traditions also maintain that the great liberation finally takes place only at the sagely level of causal/ultimate adaptation.[22,28,105] All lesser stages, no matter how occasionally ecstatic or visionary, are still beset with the primal mood of ego, which is sickness unto death. Even the saint, according to the sages, has yet to finally surrender his or her soul, or separate self sense, and this prevents the saint from attaining absolute identity with and as Godhead.[22] Since the separate self sense forms very early in development—a primitive series of ego nuclei arise within months of birth[17]—and since it does not finally uncoil until the sagely level of structural adaptation, it follows that all levels of development, short of the great liberation, are marked by the separate self.

And the separate self *is* a contraction of angst; specifically, a fear of its own death or non-being.

It was Otto Rank[73,74] who supplied the necessary psychodynamic characteristic of this state of affairs. The separate self, he said, faced with the fundamental taboo that is mortality, is forced, in order to attain a modicum of stability (translative equilibrium), to close its eyes to its own possible non-being. Put simply, it represses death ("Consciousness of death is the primary repression, not sexuality," as Becker[10] put it). One of the results of doing this, or one of the actual ways of doing this, said Rank, is by creating a series of *immortality symbols,* which, in their *promise* to transcend death, assuage the paralyzing cold that would otherwise freeze the self's operations.

If this is so, then translation deals not only with mana but with taboo, the basic taboo that is death, but a taboo that takes different and phase-specific forms on each level. From this angle, psycho-cultural productions could be seen (in part) to be *codified systems of death-denial* (I say "in part" because in my opinion that is half the truth; the other half is mana accumulation). It was Rank's genius to see that not only magic and myth but *rational* productions and purely logical beliefs were likewise immortality projects. They were productions that, in aspiring to some degree of truth, aspired to some degree of durability, and in aspiring to durability claimed hoped-for immortality ("my ideas will live on. . . ."). From that angle, culture—even rational culture—is what a separate self does with death: the self that is doomed only to die, and knows it, and spends its entire life (consciously or unconsciously) trying to deny it, both by manipulating its own subjective life and by erecting "permanent" and "timeless" cultural objects and conceptual principles as outward and visible signs of an inward and hoped-for immortality.

I will not repeat the entire argument of Rank, Becker, 51 or Brown or my reformulation of its essentials. Take, instead, a simple summary by Becker: "Man from the very beginning could not live with the prospect of death. . . . Man erected cultural symbols which do not age or decay to quiet his fear of his ultimate end. This way of looking at the doings of man gives a direct key to the unlocking of history. We can see that what people want in any epoch is a way of transcending their physical fate, they want to guarantee some kind of indefinite duration, and culture provides them with the necessary immortality symbols or ideologies; societies can be seen as structures of immortality power."

In *Up from Eden*, I tried to show some of the phase-specific forms of such death-denial. It can be the immortality promised by magic ritual: "Where there is magic, there is no death,"[23] as Campbell summarized paleolithic religion. It can be the immortality promised by myth: "To be a favorite of the gods, to be an immortal," as Becker[11] would summarize classic mythic religion. It can be the immortality promised by reason: "The god of his own thought," said L. L. Whyte,[98] "which as recompense promises immortality." There even seems to be a very subtle form of immortality project in the soul realms: the last remnant of the separate self intuits timeless Being and then mistakes that timelessness for an *everlasting duration* or *permanent* self sense ("your immortal soul," which is no such thing; the Mahayana texts are always warning practitioners not to mistake the causal-alaya for a permanent soul).[88] The point is that, until there is final liberation—if such, indeed, exists—there remains some form of immortality project. Those projects become less and less compensatory at each higher level of structural organization, but they are never fully uprooted until the separate self sense is itself uprooted. Prior to that time, life remains a battle of mana versus taboo.

In summary, the function of translation is to integrate, stabilize, and equilibrate its present level by securing
52   mana and avoiding taboo in the process of relational

exchange. This function obviously takes on different forms on different levels, but the function itself is present on all levels (functional invariant, Piaget calls it). Along with the basic deep structures, and the transformative functional invariant, this capacity seems to be part of the *native apparatus* of the self-system (cf. Hartmann's "inborn apparatus" or "undifferentiated matrix").[42]

C. Transformation: Death and Rebirth on Each Level

As we now turn to transformative or vertical development, it is a little more obvious what is involved: in order for an individual to transform to the next higher level, he or she has, in effect, to accept the *death* of the present level of adaptation, that is, to cease an *exclusive* identity with that level. Thus, for example, to progress to operational myth, the child has to give up or die to an exclusive allegiance to magical wishes; to progress to rational science, the adolescent has to give up an exclusive attachment to mythic outcomes; to progress to yogic adaptation, the adult has to surrender and release isolated-linear rationality into a larger vision-logic, and so on.[101]

In each case, it is only when the self is *strong enough to die to that level* that it can *transcend* that level, that is, transform to the next higher level of phase-specific truth, food, mana. As the self identifies with the new level and begins to adapt to its food-mana, it *then* faces the fear of dying on and to *that* level, and its translative processes swing into gear to screen out the new version of always mortality that otherwise would freeze still the movement of self. The *new* self adapts to *new* truth-mana, faces *new* other, therefore suffers new death-seizure, therefore instigates new defense measures, and therefore, among other things, erects new immortality projects.[105]

Development, in this sense, is a series of progressively shedding immortality projects by progressively shedding 53 the layers of self these projects were designed to protect, thereby simultaneously rising to new levels of phase-specific food, truth, mana. *Each* transformation is a process of death and rebirth: death to the old level, and transformation to and rebirth on the newly emergent level. And, according to the sages, when all layers of self have been transcended—when all deaths have been died—the result is only God in final Truth, and a new Destiny beyond destiny is resurrected from the stream of consciousness.

5

SOME USAGES OF
THE WORD "RELIGION"

ONE of the great difficulties in discussing religion—its
sociology, its possible universality, its "civil" dimensions—is that it is not an "it." In my opinion, "it" has
at least a dozen different, major, largely exclusive meanings, and unfortunately these are not always, not even
usually, distinguished in the literature. Let me point out
some of the ways we can (and do) use the word
"religion," and what I believe is actually behind each
usage. My point will be that each of these usages is
legitimate enough—we are free to define religion any
way we wish—but we *must specify that meaning.* For
what we will find is that many scholars have several
implicit but often very different definitions in mind, and
they slip between these usages in a way that generates
pseudo-conclusions. I will number these religious definitions and subsequently refer to them as rd-1, rd-2, and so
on.

1. *Religion as non-rational engagement.* This has
both positive and negative connotations. To theologians,
it means that religion deals with valid but non-rational
aspects of existence, such as faith, grace, transcendence,
satori, and such. To positivists, it means religion is non-

55

valid knowledge; it might be "meaningful" to humans in an emotional way, but it is not real cognition.

This usage is often reflected in common sense. Most people would intuitively say that magic-voodoo is a type of religion, however primitive, and that mythic gods and goddesses are definitely religious, although maybe not very "serious." They would also say that what yogis, saints, and sages do is certainly religious. But science-rationality? *That* is not religious. This overall usage says that religion is not so much something done on all levels but rather on particular levels, and specifically, those that are not rational-scientific per se. If you are pro-religion, then this definition implies that religion is something you can grow into; if con, something you hope to outgrow. In either case, it is non-rational; it belongs to or at least originates in a dimension that is other to reason.

2. *Religion as extremely meaningful or integrative engagement.* This usage says religion is not something that occurs on specific non-rational dimensions or levels but is a particular functional activity on any given level, an activity of seeking meaning, integration, etc. In my opinion, this usage actually reflects each level's search for mana—the search for meaning, truth, integrity, stability, and subject-object relationship (exchange). Since mana-translation, as we have seen, must occur on each level of structural organization, then whether that level appears "religious" or "secular" does not matter; it is religious, or mana-searching, by this definition.

This usage is also reflected in common sense. Thus, even the typical individual who initially says that myths, saints, sages, and such are religious but science is *not,* will usually understand exactly what you mean if you say, "Science was Einstein's religion." *Star Trek* fans say, "Logic is Spock's religion." Here, even purely rational endeavors are said to be religious, because, in my opinion, they are, like all levels, in search of their phase-

56

specific mana, and this mana-search—on *whatever* level, high or low, sacred or secular—is natively understood as religion.

Notice that, although both rd-1 and rd-2 are acceptable usages, they are nonetheless quite different, almost contradictory, and unless we specify which we mean, certain paradoxes and spurious conclusions will result. For instance, rd-1 denies secular religion, rd-2 demands it; rd-1 denies science is religion, rd-2 says it is (or can be). Both are acceptable, as long as we understand that behind the one word "religion" there are different functions. Oftentimes common sense will use both of these meanings without specifying them, thus producing a pseudo-paradox. The person might say, "Mr. Jones doesn't go to church; he doesn't believe in religion—money is his religion."

3. *Religion as an immortality project.* This is using the technical term we earlier introduced, but the actual term itself need not be invoked. The idea is simply that religion is fundamentally a wishful, defensive, compensatory belief, created in order to assuage insecurity/anxiety. This meaning is often applied to theology, but it is also used for rational and secular endeavors, as when Becker says that Marxism is Soviet religion, meaning not just mana-search (rd-2) but death-denial. This can occur, as we have seen, on any level, and simply reflects that level's inherent taboo avoidance. In this particular function, science does *for* the rational ego exactly what *myth* does for the childish ego and *magic* does for the infantile ego—helps to veil the apprehension of ultimate and inescapable mortality by providing a belief system to "hang on to." This seems especially true of "scienticians," that is, scientists whose rd-2 religion (mana religion) happens to be science itself. I have found that, when push comes to shove, they will guard their exclusively Rational World View with a quivering passion every bit as charged with hoped-for

immortality as that of a shrieking fundamentalist preacher. The point is simply that each level (short of the ultimate) tends to erect some sort of immortality project as part of its necessary defense structures, and this usage of religion simply keys on this particular function (although, typically, most of those who use this definition deny that there is any other).

4. *Religion as evolutionary growth*. This is a sophisticated concept maintaining that all evolution and history is a process of increasing self-realization, or the overcoming of alienation via the return *of* spirit *to* spirit *as* spirit. Hegel, for instance, or Aurobindo. In this sense, religion is actually a term for the transformative drive in general. The religious impulse here means, not searching for meaning, integration, mana or value *on* a given level (which is rd-2), but dying to that level altogether so as to find increasingly *higher* structures of mana-truth, eventuating in God Realized Adaptation itself.

5. *Religion as fixation/regression*. We already discussed this usage; the only thing we need say here is that this meaning differs from rd-1 only in being more specific and always derogatory. Religion is not non-rational, it is pre-rational, and that exhausts the alternatives. This is standard primitivization theory: religion is childish illusion, magic, myth.

6. *Exoteric religion*. This generally refers to the lower, outward, and/or preparatory aspects of any religion that has higher, inward, and/or advanced aspects of teaching and practise. It is usually a form of *belief* system used to invoke or support *faith*, both being preparatory to esoteric *experience* and *adaptation* (see Chapter 6 for those definitions). If a religion lacks an esoteric dimension altogether, then that religion on the whole is referred to as exoteric (the point of comparison being the esoteric dimensions of other religions).

7. *Esoteric religion.* This refers to the higher, inward, and/or advanced aspects of religious practise, with the proviso that such practises culminate in, or at least have as goal, mystical experience.

(For the next two definitions, we need a preliminary explanation. Once an author defines religion, he or she has automatically established some sort of criteria for "more valid" or "less valid" religion, simply because once the function of religion is actually specified, there are always better and worse cases. Now the nature of this "better or worse" depends upon the prior, basic definition the author gives to religion. If rd-1 is used—religion as a non-rational dimension or realm, and in this case it means higher realm—then valid religion, or more valid religion, comes implicitly or explicitly to mean actually contacting those authentic, higher realms or levels. On the other hand, if rd-2 is used—religion as search for mana on *any* level—then valid or more valid religion does not mean experiencing a particular level but finding legitimate mana on one's present level. These are obviously two entirely different meanings of "valid," and it presents a chronic semantic difficulty rarely acknowledged in the literature. I therefore have no choice but to use two different words—"authentic" and "legitimate"—to specify these two meanings of valid.)

8. *Legitimate religion.* This is religion that primarily *validates translation;* usually by providing "good mana" and helping avoid taboo, that is, providing units of meaning on the one hand and immortality symbols on the other. If an author (implicitly or explicitly) defines religion as meaningful integration of a given world view or level (rd-2), then *the more integrative* religion (within that world view or level) is implied or defined by the author to be the more valid. In these cases, since we refer to rd-2 as mana religion in general, we refer to its more valid forms as legitimate or "good mana" religion.

A *crisis in legitimacy* occurs whenever the prevailing mana and immortality symbols fail their integrative and defensive functions. This can occur on the lower levels of mythic-exoteric religion (for example, the Pope's encyclicals on human reproduction, based as they are on Thomistic/Aristotelian biological notions, long outmoded, have lost legitimacy with many people), on the middle levels of rational-secular religion (e.g., the Newtonian paradigm as a world view has lost legitimation), and on the upper levels of mystical religion (e.g., Mahayana Buddhism eventually lost legitimation in India, its place being taken by Shankara's Vedanta). In each case, the religion in its rd-2 function simply fails to provide enough meaningful integration, on the one hand, or enough immortality power, on the other, and thus loses its legitimacy, or its capacity to validate translation.

Corollary: "Degree of legitimacy" refers to the relative degree of integration, meaning-value, good mana, ease of functioning, avoidance of taboo, and so forth within any given level. This is a *horizontal scale;* "more legitimate" means more integrative-meaningful within that level.

9. *Authentic religion.* This is religion that primarily *validates transformation* to a particular dimension-level deemed to be most centrally religious. When an author (implicitly or explicitly) defines religion as a particular dimension-level of existence (rd-1), then the religion that more completely or accurately *contacts* that dimension-level is implied or defined by the author to be the more valid. In those cases, I use the word "authentic" or "more authentic" to indicate "more valid."

A *crisis in authenticity* occurs whenever a prevailing world view (or religion) is faced with challenges from a *higher-level* view. This can occur at any level, whenever a new and higher (or senior) level begins to emerge and itself gain legitimacy. The new world view embodies a new and higher transformative power and thus challenges the old view, not merely as to its legitimacy but as to its very authenticity.

Corollary: "Degree of authenticity" refers to the relative degree of actual transformation delivered by a given religion (or world view). This is a *vertical scale;* "more authentic" means more capable of reaching a higher level (and not merely integrating the present level).

An author is, of course, free to specify the nature of the centrally religious or higher realm. For myself, it is the psychic, subtle, causal, and ultimate levels of structural organization and relational exchange. It follows that, for myself, authentic religion is any theory and practise leading to a genuine emergence of, and eventual adaptation to, those realms (with the further understanding that causal religion is more authentic than subtle, which is more authentic than psychic). I will occasionally use the corollary "degree of authenticity" in a looser sense, as meaning the degree of developmental structuralization *in general* (e.g., myth is more authentic than magic, reason is more authentic than myth, vision is more authentic than reason, etc.). However, when I refer to authentic religions per se, they are ones that have reached a degree of structuralization at or beyond the superconscient border (i.e., psychic or higher). Thus, magic, myth, and reason can be (and often are) *legitimate* religions, and they can occasionally *express* authentic religious insight via peak experience (see Chapter 6). But in neither case are they the source of *authentic* religious insight, which, for me, is always and expressly *trans*-rational, not merely rational, and certainly not pre-rational.

Notice that, in very general terms, any religion (or world view) can be judged in its degree of validity on two different, independently variable scales: its degree of *legitimacy* (horizontal scale; degree of *translative* smoothness and integrity, measured against the potential capacity of the given level itself) and its degree of *authenticity* (vertical scale; degree of *transformative* power,

61

measured by the degree of hierarchical structuralization delivered by the transformation). Thus, for example, there are situations where magic, at its *full* potential (say, in some paleolithic societies) was just as *legitimate* as myth at its full potential (say, in some Bronze Age societies), but myth was more *authentic* (embodying a higher level of structural organization). If our scale of legitimacy is 1 to 10 (degree of using the integrative-mana potential of the given level) and our scale of authenticity is 1 to 10 (representing the ten levels of structuralization given in Figure 2), then in that example, the ratings would be (10, 4) and (10, 5), respectively. Here are some other examples, more commonplace:

Maoism has (or rather had) a fairly high degree of legitimacy but a very mediocre degree of authenticity. It was a *legitimate* religion (or world view) in that it apparently integrated large blocks of peoples, provided social solidarity and a measure of meaning-value, and avoided a good deal of taboo by providing the immortality ideology of an unending, never-dying people's revolution (a legitimacy rating of, say, 8–9). It was not very *authentic,* however, because it offered adaptation only to or at the mythic-rational realms (5–6); say what you will, Maoism did not produce superconscient realization of, and adaptation to, only God. Thus: Maoism (8–9, 5–6). (Notice that today Maoism has lost its legitimacy in China; the "cultural revolution" and its subsequent events were exactly a *legitimacy crisis* as defined above.) Soviet Marxism/Leninism, on the other hand, is as inauthentic as was Maoism (5–6), for the same reasons (it does not produce psychic, subtle, or causal transformation), but it also appears to be of a much lower degree of legitimacy (say, 4–5) than Maoism in its heyday, because its mana and its immortality symbols apparently have to be backed by rather large sticks.[3] So there we have examples of more or less legitimate/inauthentic (8–9, 5–6) and illegitimate/inauthentic (4–5, 5–6). (Lest my judgment seem

biased toward American-Protestant capitalism, I will
quickly add that, in my opinion, the American "civil
religion"—a mixture of exoteric, Protestant, Biblical
myths and nationalistic immortality symbols—possesses
essentially the same legitimacy and authenticity ratings as
did Maoism. That this civil religion faced a *legitimacy
crisis* during the 1960s will be discussed in Chapter 7.)

As for the authentic but illegitimate, examples abound:
when Mahayana Buddhism died in India, it was not because its tenets were per se inauthentic, for they still
embodied causal level practise (9–10), but because Vedanta Hinduism, regenerating itself via Shankara and
claiming a more historical rootedness, became more legitimate with practitioners. Likewise, Vedanta is a perfectly causal-authentic religion, but it seems it will never
achieve widespread legitimacy in America, its rating
there thus being something like (1–2, 9–10). In the West,
in fact, most esoteric spiritual tenets, no matter how authentic, never gained much legitimacy (witness Eckhart,
al-Hallaj, Giordano Bruno, Christ's esoteric-causal message itself).

As for religions that have been both legitimate and
authentic, we may take Ch'an (Zen) Buddhism during
T'ang China, Vedanta Hinduism in India from the time of
Gaudapada and Shankara to the British intensified
occupation, or Vajrayana in Tibet from Padmasambhava
to Mao Tse-tung, all of which seemed somewhere around
(8–9, 9–10).

Each of the preceding nine (or more) usages of the
word "religion" has its appropriate place—some
"religious" expressions *are* fixation/regressions, some
are immortality projects, some are mana generators,
some are legitimate, some are authentic. But we must be
careful to express precisely which usage we mean. Otherwise, statements such as "The religious impulse is univer-
63 sal," "All religions are true," "Religion is transcen-

dental," "All religions are one at some deep level," and so on are at best strictly meaningless, at worst, profoundly misleading.

6

BELIEF, FAITH, EXPERIENCE, AND ADAPTATION

In this chapter I wish to distinguish religious belief, religious faith, religious (mystical or peak) experience, and religious structural adaptation (or actual adaptation to authentic-religious levels of development). For again, if they are all "religious," they are religious to differing degrees. The series itself shows increasing religious involvement: it seems you can have belief without faith, faith without experience, and experience without complete adaptation.

A. Belief

Belief is the lowest form of religious involvement, and, in fact, it often seems to operate with no authentic religious connection whatsoever.[105] The "true believer"—one who has no literal faith, let alone actual experience—embraces a more-or-less codified belief system that appears to act most basically as a fund of immortality symbols.[10] This can be mythic-exoteric religion (e.g., fundamentalist Protestantism, lay Shintoism, pop Hinduism, etc.), rational-scientism, Maoism, civil religion, and so on. What they all have in common, when thus made a matter of "true belief," is that an ideological nexus is wedded to one's qualifications for immortality.

I believe this generates a peculiar, secondary psychodynamic: since one's immortality prospects hang on the veracity of the ideological nexus, the nexus as a whole can be critically examined only with the greatest of difficulty. Thus, when the normal and unavoidable moments of uncertainty or disbelief occur (magic: is this dance really causing rain? mythic: was the world *really* created in six days? scientistic: what happened *before* the big bang? etc.), the questioning impulses are not long allowed to remain in the self-system (they are threats to one's immortality qualifications). As a result, the disbelieving impulse tends to be *projected* onto others and then attacked "out there" with an obsessive endurance. The true believer is forever on the make, looking for converts and battling disbelievers, for, on the one hand, the mere existence of a disbeliever is one token less in the immortality account, and, on the other, if the true believer can persuade others to embrace his ideology, it helps to quiet his own disbelieving impulses. If mythic-religious, he crusades against sinners, burns witches, hangs heretics; if Marxist, he lives for the revolution that will crush disbelievers (and in the meantime jails "witches," psychiatrizes "heretics"); if scientistic, he often begins a concerted diatribe on rival (heretic) world views, even or especially those that are otherwise ridiculously insignificant (e.g., astrology, UFO, Uri Geller, Velikovsky, etc.). It is not the rightness or wrongness of the opposing view but the peculiar passion with which it is opposed that belies its origin: what one is trying to convert is one's own disbelieving self.

On the more benign side, belief *can* serve as the appropriate conceptual expression and codification of a religious involvement of any higher degree (faith, experience, adaptation). Here, belief system acts as a rational clarification of trans-rational truths, as well as the introductory, *exoteric,* preparatory "reading material" for initiates.[114] When belief systems are thus linked to actual higher (authentic) religiousness, they can be called, not because of themselves but because of association, authentic belief systems.

B. Faith

Faith goes beyond belief but not as far as actual religious experience. The true believer can usually give you all the reasons he is "right," and if you genuinely question his reasons he tends to take it very personally (because you have, in fact, just questioned his qualifications for immortality). His belief system is a politics of durability. The person of faith, on the other hand, will usually have a series of beliefs, but the religious involvement of this person does not seem to be generated solely or even predominantly by the beliefs. Frequently, in fact, the person cannot say exactly why he is "right" (has faith), and should you criticize what reasons he does give, he generally takes it all rather philosophically. In my opinion this is because belief, in these cases, is not the actual source of the religious involvement; rather, the person somehow intuits very God as being immanent in (as well as transcendent to) this world and this life. Beliefs become somewhat secondary, since the same intuition can be put in any number of apparently equivalent ways ("They call Him many who is really One"). The person of faith tends to shun literalism, dogmatism, evangelicalism, fundamentalism, which define almost solely the true believer.[13]

Paradoxically, the person of faith is often in great and agonizing religious *doubt,* which the true believer rarely experiences. The true believer has projected his doubts onto others and is too busy trying to convert them to pay attention to his own inner status. The person of faith, however, begins to transcend mere consoling beliefs and

67

thus is open to intense doubt, which the person frequently
takes to be a sign of *lack* of faith, which worries him
sorely. But that is not usually the case.

Here is what seems to occur: The person of faith intuits, although in a preliminary and somewhat vague fashion, the existence of very God. On the one hand, this
confers a measure of peace, inner stability, and a release
from mere belief. On the other hand, precisely because
that is so, the person yearns for a greater closeness to this
Divinity, a more complete knowledge-union with God.
Since the person does not yet have this greater closeness,
it throws his present state, by comparison, into *doubt* (and
yearning). In fact, *the greater the faith-intuition, the
greater the doubt.* Zen has a profound saying on this:

> Great doubt, great enlightenment;
> Small doubt, small enlightenment;
> No doubt, no enlightenment.

How different that is from the literal and dogmatic cer-
tainty of the true believer.

There seem to be only two ways fundamentally to
alleviate this doubt and yearning. One is to revert to mere
belief and clothe the doubt in more rigid and external
forms (i.e., immortality symbols). The other is to act on
the yearning and advance to experience.

C. Experience

Experience goes beyond faith into actual encounter and
literal cognition, however brief. Experience, as I am using it, means *peak experience,*[61] a temporary insight into
(and influx from) one of the *authentic* levels of religious
structural organization (psychic, subtle, causal). In my
opinion, authentic religious experience must be differentiated from mere emotional frenzy, from magical
68   trances, and from mythic mass-enthusiasms, all of which

result in a temporary suspension of reason via regression to *pre*-rational adaptations, a slide that is altogether different from *trans*-rational epiphany. Pre-rational frenzies are usually chthonic in mood, emotionally laden, body-bound, and non-insightful[105]—an emotional short-circuit that sparks and sizzles with unconscious orgiastic current. Trans-rational epiphany can be blissful, but it is also numinous, noetic, illuminative, and—most importantly—it carries a great deal of insight or understanding.[6,7]

Authentic peak experiences (as opposed to ecstatic emotional short-circuits) usually occur to those who have evolved to the rational level of structural adaptation, although occasionally they occur to those at a mythic or magic level. Actual faith seems conducive to experience; belief systems seem to inhibit it (although none of these correlations are highly positive; peak experiences are notorious for hitting just about anybody with no apparent reason).[61] When they occur to a person who previously rejected religious involvement, such experiences might effect a "conversion," with the individual subsequently adopting a particular religious belief system in order to make sense of "what hit him" (e.g., St. Paul).

If an authentic peak experience occurs to a mythic-religious true believer, it often has the awkward effect of energizing his or her mythic immortality symbols. The result is a "born-again" believer, a particularly explosive affair. To begin with, analytic experience[29,36] has consistently disclosed that the mythic true believer often possesses a particularly harsh superego (internalized aggression)—an *excessive* guilt, a *surplus* repression, often forged in the atmosphere of overly oppressive/puritanical parents. One of the reasons the mythic true believer might have become a true believer in the first place is to attempt to redress surplus guilt by establishing relations with a fictive-mythic parent who this time around would forgive the guilty transgressions (emotional-sexual impulses). At the same time, the unacceptable and guilty impulses can be projected as a world of *dirty* sinners out there. (I believe that is why a "sinner," in such cases, is usually two things: a disbeliever, or threat to the immortality account, and a "dirty" disbeliever, or contaminated with emotional-sexual guilt.)

When that type of belief system is hit with an authentic peak experience, the system *translates* it into the terms of its own immortality symbols. The whole ideology thus appears to receive a jolting sanctification; this allows the harsh superego to be extroverted, even more than usual, into a moralizing and proselytizing fury; and the true believer, now with the absolute approval of God Almighty Himself, sets out to remake the world in his own image. A *vertical* insight, usually yogic/saintly, is turned into a *horizontal* pitch forward, because the level of structural adaptation is incapable of containing and sustaining the cognitive flood.

On the other hand, but more rarely, an authentic peak experience might jolt a true believer into a person of faith, with subsequent diminution of particular-belief passion and opening of more universal tolerance.

The peak experience itself apparently can *originate* in any of the three higher realms of the person's as yet unrealized structural potentials—psychic, subtle, causal—with the precise nature of the experience differing in each case (panenhenic, theistic, monistic). It is also important to determine "into" which level of present structural adaptation the influx is "poured," since *that* seems to determine the form of its eventual expression— magical, mythical, rational.

Notice, then, that even with our simple scheme we have suggested nine substantially different varieties of authentic peak experience: psychic, subtle, or causal influx poured into magical, mythical, or rational structures. I believe I can produce ample *structural evidence* for each of these nine epiphanies, with the proviso that the more extreme pairings (e.g., magic with causal) are so structurally difficult to achieve that for all practical purposes they are nonexistent. Aside from that exception, examples from the other eight pairings are rather abundant. Typical shamanism, for instance, seems to be panenhenic magic, or psychic intuition poured into magic structures.[105] Beyond that, Joseph Campbell[23] has presented evidence that the *most advanced* and esoteric shamans understood that there was indeed one being behind the polyforms of naturic or panenhenic epiphanies—an example of theistic magic. Moses' Mt. Sinai experience seems to have been theistic mythic, or subtle level revelation flooding a mythic adaptation.[105] A modern-day Zen student's first major satori is monistic rational, or a causal-identity insight breaking into and through a rational adaptation.[88] Bertrand Russell's famous mystical experience appeared largely theistic rational, or subtle-level illumination flooding logic. On the other hand, the most common form of religious/mystical experience today seems to be yogic or panenhenic rational. The individual at a rational level of adaptation gets a "peek" experience into the psychic dimension; this is often behind everything from the "aha" or "Eureka!" experience of rational scholars to the more mundane flights of ecstatic happiness that occasionally interrupt one's purposive-rational translations.[7]

Finally, there is an esoteric or highly advanced meaning of peak experience: a person already *on* the psychic level can peak experience the subtle or causal; a person on the subtle can peak the causal. This sometimes makes it very difficult to distinguish yogic, saintly, and sagely religions, because occasionally all three will claim that all things are mere modifications of a radiant One Reality, but only the latter claims it as matter of enduring structural adaptation, the others basing the claim on mere peak experience.[7,22,105] We will now investigate that distinction.

D. *Structural Adaptation*

A peak experience, however authentic, is nonetheless merely a glimpse into those levels of structural organization that can be actually and permanently realized via higher *transformative growth* and actual structural adaptation.[101] We will, in this section, examine the implications of that view.

Prior to the modern-day influx of Eastern religions to the West, most religious scholars, psychologists, and sociologists tended to look at religion solely in terms of belief and/or faith. Largely through the influence of Eastern religion, but also due to an increased interest in Christian mysticism, neo-Platonism, and so on, the idea of *actual religious experience* (usually mystical) was added to belief and faith.

In some ways the psychologists led the field in this exploration. William James's *Varieties* was a classic investigation that concluded that the fundamental wellspring of religion was neither belief nor faith but direct experience. After all, he noted, all world religions *began* as an experience in some prophet/seer and only later were codified into belief systems that demanded faith. Carl Jung directed his investigations to the possible archetypal wellsprings of such experience, and then—relatively recently—Maslow's studies made *peak experience* the fundamental paradigm of authentic religiosity.

It has been a mixed blessing. However appropriate and necessary the peak paradigm was in helping scholars see beyond belief and faith to direct experience, the paradigm itself has blinded us to the fact that actual adaptation to these higher realms is a permanent and stable possibility and not merely a fleeting experience. A person can evolve to, for example, the saintly level of structural adaptation with the same eventual stability and continuous functioning that a person can now operate at the linguistic level.[101] We do not speak of such stable adaptations as

72

"experiences," just as we do not say, of the typical person, "He's having a linguistic experience"—he is *at* the linguistic level, *as* that level, more or less continuously.

Once we see that, beyond mere transitory experience, authentic religiosity might actually involve concrete developmental transformation and structural adaptation, then we introduce a revolution in the cognitive validity of spiritual knowledge and truth-claims. For mere belief cannot be cognitively verified, since it has no manifest referent; nor can faith, since it has no necessary content. Consequently, when psychologists and theologians introduced mystical *experience,* they thought they finally had a way to verify or cognitively ground religious claims, because experience is at least concrete. Unfortunately, it is also transitory, fleeting, impossible to replicate, privitistic, and altogether too brief to establish any claim to cognitive validity, as philosophers were very happy (and very correct) to explain.

On the other hand, if we understand that yogic, saintly, and sagely knowledge-claims are based, *not* on belief, faith, or transitory experience, but on actual levels of structuralization, cognition, and development, then the deep structures of their truth-claims assume a perfectly appropriate, verifiable, and replicable status. In fact, they would assume precisely the same *type* of status as, for example, Piaget's levels and Kohlberg's stages and could be clearly demonstrated so in the same basic way: via stage-structural analyses in any correspondingly adapted community of adequately evolved practitioners. (We will return to this topic in Chapter 9.)

I realize that the theologians are just now moving from belief and faith to experience, a move that is generating much excitement, enthusiasm, and controversy.* While all of that is a step in the right direction, I feel that its severe limitations should be kept in mind and that we

* Witness Peter Berger's *The Heretical Imperative.*

A SOCIABLE should move on, as quickly as possible, from the para-
GOD digm of peak experience to the paradigm of structural
adaptation.

7

PRESENT-DAY
SOCIOLOGY OF
RELIGION

WITH the above as background, we can quickly make a few schematic comments on various theories and topics now at the forefront of the sociology of religion.

A. *Increasing Rationalism*

Sociologists since Weber have been interested in the increasing trend toward secularization, individualism, and rationalism. In the face of the increasingly purposive-rational world view, the older mythological world views, based primarily on exoteric mythic-membership and traditional conformity, began slowly but inevitably to lose their cogency, and the very process of legitimation began to shift, in every sector, to rational adjudication and humanistic-secular appropriation. This process is far from complete, and most cultures have yet a way to go before the integrative-stabilizing forces inherent in the rational level of adaptation and organization achieve anything resembling their structural potential. But I am convinced that the mythic-membership structure has reached the inherent limit of its integrative and truth-disclosing capacities. It first emerged *c*. 9000 B.C. in certain mythic

75

farming cultures, where it slowly replaced the paleolithic magic of the great hunt; it matured in the high civilizations of classic mythology (Egypt, Shang China, Indus Valley India); and it peaked in medieval Europe under mythic-exoteric Christianity.[105] It began to die in seventeenth-century Europe; each succeeding decade has been largely defined by those persons and events that disclosed the mythic inadequacy and made plain its obsolescence: Copernicus, Newton, Locke, Nietzsche, Comte, Darwin, Freud, and so on. There are and will certainly continue to be repressions/fixations to this mode, both in individuals and societies at large, but in my opinion its force as a cogent and legitimating *translator of reality* is defunct. It can no longer provide mana of a high enough degree, and few educated individuals *can* believe its mythic immortality symbols. Like all levels of structural adaptation, it is phase-specific. Its phase has passed.

Thus, I agree with sociologists in general that the course of modern development is marked by increasing rationalization. However, my major point is that the overall trend of rationalization only covers the *first half* of our proposed developmental scheme: archaic to magic to mythic to rational. But the scheme *continues* from rational to psychic to subtle to causal to ultimate, and thus what perhaps distinguishes my viewpoint from other spiritually sympathetic theorists is that I believe the trend of rationalization per se is necessary, desirable, appropriate, phase-specific, and evolutionary. In fact, I believe it is therefore perfectly religious, *in and by itself* (no matter how apparently secular), in sense rd-4: an expression of increasingly advanced consciousness and articulated awareness that has as its final aim, and itself contributes to, the resurrection of Spirit-Geist.

I also believe rational adaptation is perfectly religious in sense rd-2: capable of providing a legitimate, cogent, integrative, and meaningful world view, or good mana (rd-8). Now, it cannot provide us with a Total World View—only causal/ultimate impact, according to the sages, can achieve absolutization.[7] But it can, I believe, provide a world view every bit as coherent and meaningful as archaic magic or syncretic myth—more so, in my opinion, for reasons we will soon investigate.

But the form of rational-individual integration is so different from that of mythic-conformity that it sometimes confuses scholars. Mythic-membership is marked by an intermediate degree of perspectivism: greater than magic, which has almost none, but not as developed as rational-reflexive, which is the first major structure to display easy and continuous perspectivism. Perspectivism itself is simply the capacity to *take the role of others,* to cognitively project oneself into a mental perspective and viewpoint other than one's own. Psychologists from Werner to Piaget have demonstrated how and why increasing perspectivism, or conversely, decreasing egocentricism, is a primary indicator of developmental evolution.[57, 70, 95] Mythic-membership ranks intermediate; it is aware of others, and can begin to take the role of others, but because it is something of a learner's stage in perspectivism, it tends to become trapped in those roles, defined by those roles, bound to them. It is thus captured by a conformist, conventional, or traditional attitude: the culture's codes are its codes, the society's norms are its norms, what they want is what I want. This is exactly Kohlberg's conventional and Loevinger's conformity stages.

With the rise of the rational level, however, the person moves into a more self-and-other reflexive, or perspectivist, position. The person can, for the first time, critically distance himself from society's norms and thus adjudicate them for himself. He can norm the norms. He might find them unworthy and reject them; he might find them honorable and embrace them, but in either case he 77 does so out of potentially reasonable and perspectivist considerations, and no longer out of blind conformity. This, of course, is Kohlberg's postconventional and Loevinger's conscientious-individualistic stages.

The paradigm of mythic-membership unity seems to be "Everybody has to think the same thing, share the same symbols, and have the same father-god-king in common." The paradigm of rational-individual unity seems to be "Let's do different things together, share different symbols, exchange different perspectives." That is still a perfectly *legitimate* form of integration or social stability; it simply does not cater to the conformity-traditional paradigm, which many sociologists seem to take as sacred. Its stability does not depend upon mythic mana, or exchange of conformity units, but on rational mana, or exchange of self-reflexive units. Mythic-membership achieves unity via shared belongingness needs; rational-individual, via shared self-esteem needs (to use Maslow's needs hierarchy). In many ways, it is potentially *more* stabilizing than mythic-membership translation because it is more resilient, more *differentiated* and *therefore* more potentially integrated. For developmental theorists, differentiation and integration are not opposites, they are complements, as when Werner summarizes: "Wherever development occurs it proceeds from a state of relative globality and lack of differentiation to a state of increasing differentiation, articulation, and hierarchical integration." Rational-individuation stands in just that relationship to the globality of mythic-membership, and it is that fact that allows scholars such as Fenn[30] and Bell[12] to point out that modern society can potentially achieve adequate stabilization without recourse to globalistic-traditionalistic units of mana. Ogilvy's *Many Dimensional Man* presents a persuasive (although very phase-specific) argument for perspectivist integrity, or unity *via* diversity, which he contrasts with the older but once appropriate integrity of one-god, one-king, one-party mentality.

If individuals at the rational level of structural adaptation choose then to pursue an *authentic* religion, as

78

opposed to the merely *legitimate* religion of secular-rationalism, they almost invariably carry their perspectivism with them and acknowledge that there are different but equally valid approaches to authentic religion—so unlike the mythic-membership believer, who, lacking sophisticated perspectivism, usually claims that his father-god-king is the only possible one and that if you want to get saved, you "got to get" membership.*

At the same time, I do not want to glorify the rational-individual level of adaptation. It is merely phase-specific. I believe it too will pass, eventually to be subsumed in a truly yogic world view. We may further suppose that, like any level, it can translate its world sanely or morbidly, provide good mana or bad. There seems to be "good" and "bad" reason just as there is "good" and "bad" mythology. But in my opinion we should not take the worst of reason, compare it with the best of mythology, and then claim reason itself, or the level of differentiated-individuated rational adaptation, is a degenerate structure in contrast to yesterday's "really religious," Garden-of-Eden, mythic-conformity modes.

My point is that religious scholars have often seen the trend toward rationalization and concluded that it is an anti-religious trend, whereas for me it is a *pro-authentic-religious* trend by virtue of being trans-mythic or post-mythic and *on its way to* yogic and higher levels of structural adaptation. If indeed rationality is the great divide between subconscient magic and myth and super-conscient subtle and causal, then its major purpose in the overall scheme of evolution might be to strip Spirit of its infantile and childish associations, parental fixations, wish fulfillments, dependency yearnings, and symbiotic gratifications. When Spirit is thus de-mythologized, it can be approached *as* Spirit, in its Absolute Suchness (*tathata*), and not as a Cosmic Parent.

---

* For an excellent discussion of modern sociological pluralism/perspectivism, see Berger's *The Heretical Imperative*.

When asked to explain the religious world view that rationalization is supposedly "destroying," such scholars almost always point to magic or mythic symbologies, thereby elevating pre-rational structures to a trans-rational status. Since development *does* move from pre-rational myth to rational discourse to trans-rational epiphany,[102] then if one confuses authentic religion with myth, naturally rationalization *appears* anti-religious. If, however, authentic religion is seen to be trans-rational, then the phase-specific moment of rational-individuation is not only a step in the right direction, it is an absolutely necessary prerequisite.

B. Robert Bellah

In my opinion, the greatest contribution of Bellah's work, other than being marked at every turn by immense clarity and perception, is his rigorous demonstration that in some sense religion should be treated as religious, that is, non-reductionistically. This started a minor revolution in modern sociology. Beyond that, however, I have a few reservations.

1. In treating all religious expressions "non-reductionistically," Bellah tends to lose any serious critical capacity (see Chapter 1, section C, Phenomenological-Hermeneutics). Indeed, when he says "religion is true," he abandons the position of *profound* developmental possibilities and overlooks the hierarchy of truth capacities. One might as well say "morality is true" and then overlook the extraordinary differences—including the increasingly *higher* nature—of the half-dozen or so stages of moralization discovered by modern developmental psychology.

This lack of vertical critical dimension, under what often seems to me a questionable use of "non-reductionism," not only overlooks the possible hierarchy of authentic religious adaptation—yogic, saintly, sagely—it takes at close to face value any apparently religious symbol ("symbolic realism") and thus accords eminent status to what might simply be childish fixations. Reductionism, in my opinion, rightly refers to trying to explain *higher* domains by *lower* ones (mind by instinct, subtle by mind, etc.), and that is indeed deplorable. Bellah, however, does not systematically distinguish higher and lower; reductionism thus comes to mean saying anything about a domain other than what it wishes to say about itself. Especially, Bellah does not distinguish pre-rational "religion" from trans-rational religion and thus, in trying to protect the latter from reductionism, he often must glorify the former.

2. Bellah's background definition of religion is that which serves the holistic interrelation of subject and object in a meaningful way. This is basically rd-2: religion as the relational exchange of mana (on whatever level). It is with this definition that Bellah can (correctly) say that all societies are religious, even secular ones, and that all religions (in that sense) are true. And because he is generally working with rd-2, his criteria of "more valid" religion is rd-8: a more integrative religion is a more valid, useful, or meaningful one. The criteria here is that of *legitimacy*. For example, the American "civil religion" (a mixture of mythic Protestant ethic and American nationalistic immortality symbols) is or was a legitimate religion, according to Bellah, because it provided adequate integrative-meaning, moral restraint, and social cohesion. I agree that that is so. The civil religion was a good mana generator and taboo avoider; it was a legitimate religion (in the rd-8 sense).

However, because of his non-critical ("non-reductionistic") stance, Bellah fails to distinguish systematically between such merely legitimate religions and *authentic* religions. Thus, he will say things like, "The civil religion at its best is a *genuine apprehension of universal*

81

and transcendental reality. . . ."[13] Now, say what you
will, civil religion per se, even at its best, did not produce
anything resembling real satori, moksha, or *genuine apprehension* of very Spirit. This obfuscation occurs, in my
opinion, because Bellah confuses legitimate mana
religion—what should happen on all levels of structural
adaptation—with authentic-transcendent religion, which
happens only on the upper levels of structural adaptation.

3. On occasion, however, Bellah will also use religion
as rd-1; for various reasons, he has a specific dimension-
realm in mind when he says "religion," and that realm,
whatever else it is, is not scientific-rational. Thus he will
say, "It is in this sense religious, not scientific."[13] That is
a perfectly acceptable usage of religion, as we have seen;
it is rd-1.

In my opinion, Bellah is here attempting to refer not
merely to a *legitimate* religion, which even secular-
rational society can be, but also to an *authentic* religion,
which is beyond or trans to rational-individuation (and
which, therefore, Bellah is understandably reluctant to
grant to scientific-secular societies; in my opinion, they
may be legitimate but are not authentic). But in failing
systematically to distinguish between trans-rational and
pre-rational domains, Bellah extends *authenticity* to pre-
rational, mythic engagements and civil religions,
whereas they possessed at most a sturdy *legitimacy*. Now
scientific-rational society is, for a variety of reasons,
today facing various sorts of legitimation crises itself, and
these are an important topic of investigation and criticism. But in my opinion, Bellah confuses the present-
day loss of legitimation, which civil and mythic religions
had, with a loss of *authenticity* that they *never* possessed.
He thus laments: "So-called postreligious man, the cool,
self-confident secular man that even some theologians
have recently celebrated, is trapped in a literal and circumscribed reality that is classically described in re-

ligious terms as the world of death and sin, the fallen world, the world of illusion. Postreligious man is trapped in hell."[13]

What Bellah calls "postreligious" is simply postmythic and postconventional. And, as we suggested in the last section, postmythic men and women are not post-authentic-religious, but pre-authentic-religious, poised at the rational level of structural adaptation, ready for the next overall step in collective development and the *first* step in authentic, collective, spiritual experience—that of widespread yogic adaptation. Trapped in hell? Most definitely, as are *all* stages short of superconscient resurrection. But the point is that the previous mythic-religious men and women were equally trapped in hell; in fact, more so; they simply had not the high degree of rational-reflexive awareness necessary to thoroughly realize their plight, and thus suffered their misery in relative innocence, allowing what qualms as might surface to be suckled by a mythic cosmic parent. *That* covenant needed to be broken.

They are indeed still trapped in hell, as were their predecessors, but postmythic men and women have at least, and finally, thrown off their childish images of deity as a protective parent sniveling over their every move, listening to their every wish-fulfillment, catering to their every immortality project, dancing to their prayers of magic. Postmythic men and women did not get thrown out of Eden; they grew up and walked out, and, in now assuming rational and personal responsibility for a measure of their own lives, stand preparatory for the next great transformation: the God within, not the Father without.

4. Finally, Bellah maintains that religion, unlike science, has no verifiable (testable) cognitive truth-claim. I disagree with this strongly, for reasons suggested in Chapter 6 and discussed again in Chapter 9.

C. *Anthony and Robbins*

Dick Anthony and Thomas Robbins have recently moved to correct what they see as some of the weaknesses and contradictions in Bellah's theories, principally by replacing (or supplementing) symbolic realism with structuralism, and specifically a structuralism modeled on Chomsky's deep and surface patterns.

I am obviously in sympathy with the main thrust of their work, and I can recommend its general features with enthusiasm. Here, I would simply like to suggest a few minor amendments to their presentations in light of our discussion thus far.

1. Anthony and Robbins[3] begin by suggesting that Bellah's approach to religion, which sees it as a universal and non-reducible *factum* of human existence, is a start toward a long-sought formulation of "universal structural principles intrinsic to religion," that is, "Symbolic realism seems to imply a fundamental unity of all religions at a deep level." They point out, however, that Bellah fails to carefully distinguish between the deep structures of such universal religion, which would be everywhere invariant and a-historical, and the surface structures of religion, which would be everywhere variable and contingent. Consequently, they note, "Bellah's recent work has emphasized two trends that, on the face of it, seem contradictory. In his metatheoretical papers, he has stressed the underlying uniformity of seemingly diverse religious traditions and epochs. However, in his actual description of concrete religious systems, Bellah has emphasized the necessity of religious change [and] religious evolution. . . ." Anthony and Robbins then argue that

the apparent contradictions between these positions arise because Bellah has not made explicit the distinction between the surface structure and deep structure of religions. When he emphasizes the similarities in religions of different cultures and epochs, he is focusing upon what should properly be called the deep structure of religion. When he focuses upon the changes in religion relative to changing psychological, sociological, and economic conditions, he is describing surface structures.

As cogent as that argument for deep and surface structure is (we will return to it enthusiastically in a moment), the failure to make that distinction is not primarily the cause of "the apparent contradictions" in Bellah's work. Bellah does not, it is true, explicitly make that important distinction, but *prior* to that omission, in my opinion, is the more fundamental lack of distinction between legitimate and authentic religions, *each* class of which has representative deep and surface structures. For example, there is the deep structure of magic religion (marked by confusion of symbol and thing symbolized, condensation, diplacement, etc.), and there are actual surface manifestations of magic religion (voodoo here, naturic animism there, Bon religion here, and so on). There is the deep structure of causal religion (marked by unmanifest absorption, identity of self and absolute ground, etc.), and there are actual surface manifestations of causal religion (Zen, Vedanta, Eckhart, etc.). And so with each class. If these levels of structural realization are not first distinguished, then any merely legitimate religion may be confused with genuinely authentic religion, and the *dynamics* of legitimacy may be likewise confused with the *dynamics* of authenticity. That is, what happens at each level of the spectrum of existence (universal or ever-present need for mana, meaning) might be confused with what specifically defines the *higher* levels of the spectrum (actual universal mysticism), with the result that what we mean by "deep" and "surface" structures is skewed from the start, most often by having "deep" mean authentic (or mystical) and "surface" mean legitimate, instead of seeing that authentic religions have deep and surface structures, legitimate religions have deep and surface structures, and the two do not necessarily overlap.

85

Let me give as a correlative example Maslow's work on the hierarchy of needs, which are: physiological needs (material), safety needs (magic-body protective), belongingness needs (mythic-membership), self-esteem needs (rational-reflexive), self-actualization needs (psychic), and the self-transcendence needs (subtle-causal).[61] Now we can say *need is universal*, or ever-present, which of course it is, because it occurs on *all* levels. But that "need-as-universal" is not to be confused with *the* need for universal-mystical self-transcendence, which occurs on the *highest* levels. Just so, if we define religion as meaning-need (rd-2), then of course it is universal and occurs on all levels, as mana search, and we can further investigate what constitutes *good* mana on all levels (rd-8), so as to trace out the actual *dynamics* and possible functional invariants, cross-level, of legitimation itself. But if by religion we *also* wish somehow to convey, as Anthony and Robbins appropriately do, a meaning of authentic or universal-mystical union (and *philosophia perennis*), then only the highest and transcendent levels are directly involved.

Those are two completely different (but equally important) forms of "universal religiousness" or "universal structural principles intrinsic to religion," principally because they reflect two quite different forms of religion (rd-2 and rd-1) and correlative validity scales (rd-8 and rd-9, or legitimacy and authenticity). The former is a universality of all good-mana religion at some deep level, "deep level" here meaning the functional similarities and dynamics of all legitimately integrative-horizontal translations. The latter is a "transcendental unity" reached and shared only by those rather rare sub-sects of certain religions that actually embrace an authentically mystical or *esoteric* level, or the superconscient realm in general, which is what scholars of the *philosophia perennis* mean by the phrase "transcendent unity of religions." Bellah's work deals basically with the former, or legitimate mana and immortality symbols (which is why I think he speaks so highly of Norman O. Brown's works). Anthony and Robbins wish to make more explicit room for the latter, or authentic mystical religion, but—in failing to explicitly distinguish legitimate and authentic—they generally try to make the former a surface structure of the latter as deep structure. They consequently overlook the possibility that mysticism per se (panenhenic, theistic, or monistic) is the deep structure of which *only* the authentic religions (yogic, saintly, or sagely) are surface structures. For, in my opinion, actual mysticism is no more the deep structure of, for example, civil religion, than the self-transcendence need is the deep structure of, for example, the safety needs.

In other words, Anthony and Robbins significantly improve Bellah's ideas by introducing deep and surface structures to his formulations, but they tend to simply reproduce his confusion of legitimate and authentic religions, the confusion of legitimate mana on any level with authentic mana on the mystical levels, the confusion of universal functional invariants of good integration with universal mystical integration. They then take the deep structure of authentic mysticism (or divine immanence) and instead of assigning it its own *authentic* surface structures, assign it any merely *legitimate* surface structures from any lower level, no matter how otherwise completely lacking in authenticity they might be. It is in this vein that they say, for example, "Maoism shares certain universal features of traditional religions (and thus *is* a religion in our sense), whereas Russian communism does not. . . ."[3] These features, which Maoism supposedly possesses, Anthony and Robbins wish explicitly to connect to the deep structure of "an inner experience of ultimate reality."[3] In other words, the deep structure of authentic mysticism is supposed to underlie the surface structure of legitimate Maoism. Again, I think it is obvious that the experience of Maoism and the experience of

87

samadhi are not related as surface and deep structures but as two different levels of structuralization altogether. Better to say that Maoism is a *legitimate* religion (surface structure) at the mythic-to-rational level (deep structure), whereas Russian communism is still struggling for similar legitimacy at the same level, but *neither* are *authentic* religions, as are, for example, Vedanta and Zen, which are two different but more or less legitimate surface structures (in India and Japan, respectively) of the *same* causal-level deep structure.

At the same time, one can compare all types of *legitimate* religions, whether also authentic or not—say, Maoism, American civil religion, Vajrayana in pre-communistic Tibet, exoteric Shi'ite Islam—in order to determine what they have in common ("deep structure" in an entirely different sense) as good integrators of societies, and thus discover and formulate the dynamics and basic functional invariants of "healthy" religion. I have already suggested that such dynamics would include good mana production and taboo avoidance (via meaning-units and immortality symbols). Such "deep structures," in their potential form, would also probably be native, as explained for translative potentials in Chapter 4. Lack of authenticity would then be related to lack of *transformative* symbology; lack of legitimacy, to lack of adequate *translative* symbology, itself related in part to a failure of transcription, or adequate read-out of the potentials available to the particular level.

In summary, if the distinction deep/surface is made without the prior distinction of authentic/legitimate, then one of the results is that *authentic* mysticism may appear to be the deep structure of which all lower and merely *legitimate* religions are supposed to be surface structures, instead of seeing that each level has its own deep and surface structures, that surface structures can function legitimately or illegitimately on every level, that only on the highest levels does authentic mystical union manifest itself, and that the deep structures of those mystical levels—psychic, subtle, causal—have as surface structures only the religions evoking them—yogic, saintly, sagely.

2. Anthony, in an important paper ("A Phenomenological-Structuralist Approach to the Scientific Study of Religion"[2]), the merits of which I will emphasize in a moment, again suggests "convergence of lines of evidence pointing toward *universal mysticism* as the data base for the deep structure component of . . . a two-level [deep/surface] structuralist theory of religion." Now we have already suggested that universal mysticism is *not* the deep structure of lower-level legitimate religions, such as magic-voodoo, exoteric mythic religion, Maoism, civil religion, for they take as deep structure the intrinsic rules and patterns that define and govern the particular (lower) level of structural adaptation on which their existence is grounded.

But what I wish specifically to emphasize in this section is that even when we understand that actual mysticism is the deep structure of only authentic religious experience-adaptation, we still have to be careful to differentiate the hierarchical *types* of mystical union. There are at least three or four types, as we have seen, and each has a *deep structure* (psychic, subtle, causal, or ultimate) that underlies various *surface structures* of authentic religious symbology (e.g. and respectively, Tundra Shamanism, Mosaic Judaism, Vedanta Hinduism, Maha Ati Vajrayana), authentic religious practice (e.g. and respectively, hatha-yoga arousal, shabd or interior prayer-contemplation, jnana-insight or radical absorption in the Heart, and sahaja or ultimate-spontaneous Identity), and authentic mystical unions (panenhenic, theistic, monistic, non-dual).

My own feeling is that even this four-level hierarchy will soon be replaced with a much more complex one, 89 containing up to a dozen discrete developmental structures. But in any event, the old notion that there are only two types or levels of religion—exoteric, which is everywhere different, and esoteric, which is everywhere identical—is about as precise as saying there are two forms of mental cognition, primary and secondary. That early Freudian division is acceptable enough, but we can be much more precise: for example, Piaget's description of four structure-stages, which is, of course, exactly the type of refinement I believe will happen with both exoteric *and* esoteric religions.

But the real reason I mention Anthony's paper is that, aside from these small amendments, I believe it is packed with all the right insights and suggestions for a general structural approach to religion. There is no need of my merely repeating his contributions here; I suggest the reader consult the paper itself, for the essentials of his suggestions are surely ones we will want to include in a well-rounded approach to religion.

3. The refinements I have suggested might also allow us to tease apart the idea that only surface structures change in religious history while deep structures remain everywhere monolithic. Now it is true that a deep structure in itself is a-historical, but it *emerges* in the course of history, and we can trace those revolutionary emergences. On the other hand, when it is thought that there is only *one* basic deep structure of religion, then naturally that deep structure must also be assumed to have been present from the earliest religious expression, and so all religious history is pictured as a mere shuffling of various surface structures around this "single," "universal" deep structure. But once we see that there might be four or more major deep structures of authentic religion (not to mention exoteric religions), then it becomes more than probable that the history of religion involves not only evolution of surface structures but also

revolution in deep structures.

Stated differently, most religions, in the course of their histories, seem to face various *legitimation crises,* usually prompted by various rival surface structures. But occasionally a particular religion might face what amounts to an *authentication crisis:* it either fails to provide the actual *transformation* that it promised, or it is faced with a religion that delivers higher-level transformation altogether. For example, at least two such significant transformations in the West seem to have occurred[105]: (1) The transformation from a somewhat crude yogic-shamanistic and panenhenic worship to a truly subtle and saintly involvement, epitomized perhaps by Moses, who, according to legend, descended from Mt. Sinai to directly challenge such "nature worship"; and (2) The transformation from Mosaic saintly worship to causal identity, epitomized by Christ and al-Hallaj, both of whom were murdered "because you, being a man, make yourself out God."

These religion-transformational crises and conflicts are, I believe, simply a subset of what happens at every level of development as a new and higher structure emerges to replace or subsume the prior and lower. My point is simply that, in the study of religious development (as a subset of general developmental principles), we might be sensitive to the differences in historico-dynamics between surface structure rivalries and deep structure revolutions, between legitimation crises and authentication crises.

D. The New Religions

There is an abundance of literature dealing with the new religious movements in America; they seem to be the acid test of a sociological theory. In this section I will apply the theory of transcendental sociology in outline form.

91

1. We can again begin with Bellah's work, for I think his analysis of American civil religion is cogent. I disagree that it was an authentic religion, but it seemed most definitely a legitimate religion: it served good mana on a mythic-membership level and it offered an easy abundance of immortality symbols. According to Bellah (and others), the American civil religion fatally hemorrhaged in the 1960s, and the new religions, in various forms, are in large measure the result. What follows—the rest of section D,1—is my *opinion* of what happened.

The old civil-religious, traditional-membership covenant was already under strain due to increasing rationalization and consequent (healthy) de-mythologizing; what legitimation it had left was finally broken under the combined onslaught of radical student politics, post-conventional rationality, Viet Nam, alternative (Eastern) spiritual epiphanies, economic doubts, and a general debunking of American nationalism. As the old translation-covenant finally disintegrated, it left in its wake *three separate lines of development,* lines that were already in existence to some degree but now stood naked in their form and accelerated in their pace.

a. The sector of ongoing secular-rationalization, which has now dominated the universities, the media, most central political-technical steering decisions, the intelligentsia, and the world view of most educated, liberal individuals.

b. A very small sector that, already brought up in an atmosphere of increasing rational-secularism and more or less adapted to it, began to search for, or actually develop to, literal yogic structuralization. Interest in Eastern yogic and meditative disciplines, Christian mysticism, and certain new forms of intensive psychotherapy, were evidence of a thirst for such trans-rational saturation. *However,* not all, not even most, individuals interested in the "new religions" were authentically ready for actual trans-rational and yogic adaptation, because

C. The broken covenant found a large sector of the population unready and unable to transform to responsible, postmythic, rational individuality (let alone trans-rational yogic discipline). This was exacerbated by the uncontested fact that the (horizontal) developmental course of rational-individuation was not itself operating up to its integrative potential: it was not providing the good mana it is structurally capable of. Thus, for various reasons, a significant number of individuals were alienated from the rational-individual society that was rapidly if precariously emerging. In search of some sort of legitimate mana (integrative truth), some of these individuals took regressive consolation in various pre-rational immortality symbols and mythological ideologies. These were largely of two sorts.

(1) Fundamentalistic mythic religion: a new surge in exoteric Protestant mythology, complete with proselytizing fury, evangelical non-perspectivism, saved-by-the-father (Oedipal) immortality symbols, patriarchal sexism, and authoritarian obedience. Largely composed of true believers, this sector, basically, wanted to put the broken covenant back together again.

(2) Cultic new age religions: such as the Moonies, Hare Krishna, Jesus freaks, and so forth; these are essentially *identical* in deep structure with the fundamentalist mythic religion of the evangelicals, but their drastically different surface structures have the all-important advantage of allowing one, in such cults, to express disaffection with both rational society *and* one's parents, should one's parents already be expressing disaffection with rationality via mythic revivals. Dressing up like a Hindu can both scream disapproval of society at large and really get to your own fundamentalist Christian parents; even better, dress up like Jesus Christ.

93

My point is simply that "the" new religions really involve at least two drastically different structural celebrations: trans-rational, on the one hand, and pre-rational, on the other. The former is primarily (but not solely) a manifestation of ongoing postrational development, vertical transformation, and higher structuralization, whereas the latter is largely (but not solely) a product of failure at rational-individuation (exposed when the covenant broke) and a regression/fixation to pre-rational, mythic, and even occasionally archaic-magical (Manson, Jim Jones) structural disadvantages.[102]

2. There remains the possible role that the authentic mystical sector ("b" above) might have in actual large-scale societal transformation. For our general paradigm of revolutionary (not merely evolutionary) change is as follows: the present translation begins to fail its soothing, phase-specific integrative tasks, that is, its units of meaning no longer command common sense; too many of its immortality symbols have shockingly suffered damage (death); structural tension begins to increase, driving the system into various turmoils and perturbations; the structure eventually begins to loosen and break; if there are no viable seed crystals in the old translative repertoire, the system either regresses to lower forms or completely disintegrates; if there are viable seed crystals, then the structural tensions are absorbed and channeled through those crystals, and the system as a whole escapes its conflicts into a higher level of structural organization and integration. The old translation dies; transformation ensues; new and higher translations are born.

So where do we look for these seed crystals? Where are the enclaves and harbingers of future transformation? By definition-paradigm, they are most likely in those sectors now deemed "out-law" by the laws and in-laws of the present translation. Robbins and Anthony[77] quote Tir-

yakian,

If we accept the notion that social revolutions essentially involve a fundamental re-ordering of the social structure, and if we accept the supposition that the social order is essentially viewed as a moral phenomenon by the members of the collectivity, then there must be a new source of morality involved in societal change, one that both desacrilizes the present system and paves the way for the acceptance of a new order. (This is the death and rebirth aspect of social revolutions [we have already examined this death/rebirth aspect of all forms of transformation; see Chapter 4, C].) Since established religion represents a compromise with the ongoing secular institutions, the only other possible host of revolutionary thought, however unwittingly, is the non-institutionalized religious sector. . . .

Thus, concludes Tiryakian, "important ideational components of change (i.e., changes in the social consciousness of reality) may often originate in the non-institutionalized ["out-law"] groups or sectors of society whose paradigms of reality may, in certain historical moments, become those which replace institutionalized paradigms and become in turn new social blueprints."

I believe such statements are true, but it would help if we could be more specific. For notice that although all future truths are now contained in out-laws (by definition), not all out-laws are truthful (just as in science only the theories that today seem absurd *can* be the truths of tomorrow, but not all absurd theories are therefore true—most are, in fact, absurd, today and tomorrow). Just so with social "absurdities": in the class of general out-laws in any society, there are pre-laws, counter-laws, and trans-laws, and apparently their influences on social revolutions are completely different.

Pre-laws are those individuals who, for various reasons, are not able or do not wish to rise to the average expectable level of structural adaptation of a given society. They often end up in jails (as blatant anti-laws) or mental institutions, although frequently their pre-conventional structuralization is benign enough and simply adds, for want of a better metaphor, salt to societal stew. But it should be noted that *most* of the teachings and practices that call themselves "esoteric" or "occult" are, in my opinion, pre-law; they are thinly rationalized magic, *not* psychic and *not* saintly. Astrology, tarot, "magick," voodoo, festival ritual, and such largely follow exactly the deep structure of magical/primary process cognition, and they—along with other forms of pre-law, pre-conventional consciousness—are *not* seed crystals of the future, unless that future spells regression.

Counter-laws make up the largest portion of what is loosely called "counterculture." Neither pre-law nor trans-law, counter-law is the precise mirror image of the present law. It is largely composed of adolescentlike mentality, which, in a phase-specifically appropriate enough fashion, attempts to establish individual identities by taking each facet of present law and either acting out its precise *converse* (e.g., short-hair society produces long-hair counterculture) or its precise *caricature* (prove mastery of it and thus independence from it by "hamming it up," although this is initially an unconscious posturing and thus is performed with monumental seriousness; e.g., Mom and Dad drink, I'll be a drunk). If either of these tendencies is overblown, the counter-law becomes an anti-law (and is usually jailed). In general, however, "Counterculture may be described," says Marin, "as the tribalized, ritualized, mirror of national culture."[59]

Notice in particular that when authentic yogic-saintly religions are introduced to counter-laws, those disciplines are merely *translated* into the terms of the struggle for adaptation at adolescent rationality (i.e., counter-rationality). Such otherwise authentic disciplines thus end up embodying, via caricature, all of the predominant values of the present laws and translations of society. In this particular case, "New spiritual patterns, like the sixties counterculture, do not really challenge or antithesize dominant cultural patterns, but rather reflect and elabo-

rate those patterns, including consumerism, individualism, spiritual privitism, and a fetishism of 'techniques.'"[77] Counter-laws can take authentic spiritual practises and turn them into caricatured thrills, "so self-centered," says Bellah, "that they begin to approximate the consumer cafeteria model."[78]

This is not to say these counter-law movements are therefore trivial; they are not transformative, but they do seem to serve a useful function for *present* society: they help forward and stabilize the given translations of the society by allowing its members, especially adolescent-phasers, to embrace its dominant values while pretending not to, thus accomplishing necessary socialization and individuation at once. In allowing its counter-laws to stand out in theory, it tucks them in in fact. Failure to grasp that elemental point has led more than one scholar to mistake counter-laws for trans-laws and proclaim the greening of America, the aquarian new age, and so on.

So far, we have discussed pre-laws and counter-laws (and possible anti-laws): The pre-laws are a relatively regressive sector, either trapped in or exploiting levels of structural organization lower than the present, average expectable level of societal translation. Their effect is per se disintegrative; however, in small numbers, and especially in their more benign modes, they may contribute to the overall translative integration of society by forming sub-societies that answer their own needs and thus spare society the disruption. Should this sector assume significant proportions, however, it generally becomes a source (or a symptom) of what can only be called "decadence," and if society at large finds its own higher-level translations burdensome, a truly disintegrative-regressive trend can result. The classic example, apparently, is Rome.

The counter-laws, on the other hand, usually serve the overall translative integration of society by embracing its fundamental values via a converse-caricatured rehearsal that simultaneously allows the necessary process of individuation and post-conformist moralization. This seems to be the basis of the swing in styles with each generation; Eisenhower parents produced student radicals who now, as parents, are giving birth to little Republicans. What occasionally can result within this counter-swing is a more benign re-arrangement of the present translations; for example, student protests sometimes *are* legitimate protests.

The point is that neither pre-laws nor counter-laws seem to be significant sectors of actual social *transformation*—not on the emergent scale we are now discussing. (All sorts of "translative revolutions" are also possible, of course, especially in material modes of production, technological innovations, etc. These, however, do not necessarily involve actual transformations in structures of consciousness.) If actual social transformations do generally come from some sort of presently out-lawed sector, the only one left to consider is that of the yogic trans-laws. It would be helpful, then, if we could specify more precisely the type of yogic seed crystals that might give birth to the eventual transformation, because merely being a trans-law, however authentic, does not ensure being the eventually *legitimate* catalyst of a given transformation.

Perhaps we can surmise where we will find the major future catalysts by looking at the structure-stage they will replace. For, in my strongest opinion, before a true yogic transformation can occur, rational-individual society will first have to reach its full potential and provide the phase-specific truths, values, and substructures for which it is designed and upon which future transformations will depend, such as appropriate technology, a sophisticated medical base, telecommunications as global bonding via global perspectivism, computer interfacing as an extension of mind, and especially a de-mythologizing of reality, divinity, and consciousness.

98

It follows that, in my opinion, the first *large-scale* transformative trends will come through those who have already adequately mastered that rational-individuated-operative base. For yogic insight comes *through* and then out of the realm of reason, not around it or away from it or against it. They will come from within, these yogis. They might have first flirted with yogic philosophy during their adolescent counter-law phase, but they will have subsequently come to terms with the law itself and therefore will be in a firm position to consciously move beyond it and not merely unconsciously react to it.

Whether esoteric, mystical, nonfundamentalist Christianity will be able to carry out this transformation, or whether it can even survive the prior, necessary demythologizing and dismantling of its exoteric, patriarchal, mythical accouterments, I do not know. (For a superb account of what this new/renewed Christianity would have to look like, see Jacob Needleman's *Lost Christianity*.) But I am fairly convinced that one of the keys to the specific *type* of future transformation lies in *surface structure compatibility,* that is, in a compatibility of the old and new translations, a *bequeathing of legitimacy* (the old and new have to be different enough to constitute an actual transformation, but similar enough to encourage people to jump, as it were). Therefore, the new yogic translations will likely have certain surface structures that are compatible with (and perhaps occasionally direct continuations of) past surface structure symbolizations. For example, the modern phase of rational-individuation, however otherwise different from its mythic-Christian predecessor, retains an emphasis on personhood and individuality, which is clearly Judaeo-Christian in origin and nature (God loves and protects individual souls; the individual person is cherished in the eyes of the Lord; God Himself is a big person, so is His Son, etc.).

99

Because of this general necessity for surface structure compatibility, I do not believe that Eastern religions will serve as large-scale models for Western transformation, however otherwise significant they might have proven to be in terms of being provocateurs. Their influence will be considerable, to be sure, but in a way that is finally translated and assimilated in the new Western yogic world view, and not merely transplanted *en bloc*. Therefore, if the yogic transformation is not esoterically Christian, it would not surprise me if a new and specifically Western mysticism arose, although it would be compatible in surface terms with Christian symbology *and* rational technology. (To give a silly example, but one I have already heard elsewhere: yogic meditation is called "a psychotechnology of contemplative love." In the same vein, notice three phenomena whose deep structure is often that of mystical impulse but whose surface structures are such that they could initially have arisen almost nowhere but in America: biofeedback, widespread LSD use, and *A Course in Miracles*. Those are in some ways authentic yogic-saintly endeavors that became very popular because of *surface structure compatibility* with, respectively, American technology, American drug-oriented medicine/culture, and American fundamentalistic-Protestant belief in magic prayer.) My point is simply that the new Western mysticism will say all the right things, use all the right symbols, cater to all the old desires, and it will begin to remake the Western world.

3. The three great domains of human development—childish subconsciousness, adolescent self-consciousness, and mature superconsciousness—are each marked by a dominant psychological attitude: passive dependence, active independence, and actively passive surrender (they stand in the relationship thesis, antithesis, synthesis).[101,93] The point of this section is that the first and last attitudes are often confused by scholars, a confusion that results in certain mistaken conclusions on the nature of spiritual community.[102]

Passive dependence is the disposition of the infant-child self-system, simply because it is not yet developed enough to assume responsibility for the relational exchanges of its basic mana-needs (physiological, safety, belongingness). It depends for its very existence on specific relational exchanges with specific partners: mother, father, significant others. Due to its fledgling boundaries, it is especially open to traumatic displacements, splitting, fragmentation, dissociation. These distortions are particularly significant for future development, because (as outlined in Chapter 3, B) they tend to reproduce themselves on the higher levels of structural organization as the latter emerge and consolidate. Like a grain of sand caught in the early layers of a pearl, each successive layer is crinkled and weakened at a stress point that keeps reproducing itself. Such stress points for the young self-system especially concern its relation to disciplinary or authority figures, since for the most part this actually represents the relation between its own lower and pre-verbal structures, especially emotional-sexual and aggressive impulses, and its fledgling symbolic-verbal and mental structures, one of whose jobs will be to subdue and transform the emotional-vital components into higher expressions. That is, the interpersonal relation between child and parent is also the intrapersonal relation between the child's own body and mind. Neither relationship can the child yet master, and thus both basically highlight the child's fundamental mood of passive dependence.

All of which changes, or can change, with the emergence in adolescence of the critical, self-reflexive, self-conscious mentality.[54,66,101] The adolescent rebellion against the parents is largely an outward symptom of the inner (and healthy) fight to differentiate from or transcend childish dependence and magic-mythic subconsciousness. The pre-law of the child gives way to the counter-law of the adolescent. There is a corresponding swing in mood from general passive dependence to active indepen-

101

dence (again, this *can* go too far, from counter-law to anti-law, but by and large it is nothing but a healthy differentiation and transformation).

The adolescent mood of active independence is a phase-specific form of transcendence—the transcendence from subconscious dependence to self-conscious responsibility.[101] But if it persists beyond its phase-specific moment—which in most Western cultures it does—it acts merely to *prevent* the emergence of the mature disposition of an actively passive surrender of isolated individuality to its own higher and prior nature, or radical superconsciousness, in and as the entire world process at large. This is a *surrender,* in that adolescent swaggering has to be released—died to—in order to make room for rebirth on the superconscient levels. It is *passive,* in that the center of squirming impatience known as ego must eventually relax its chronic contraction in the face of a wider awareness. And it is *actively* passive because it is no mere trancelike submission, but entails an effort of keenest concentration, perception, and will to cut through the obsessive rationalization and stream of contracted thought that constitutes ego. In the gesture of actively passive surrender, the higher centers of superconscient potential are *actively* engaged, the ego is rendered open and *passive,* and consequently the egoic self sense can relax into, and *surrender* as, the wider currents of being and awareness that constitute the goal and ground of its own development—a surrender that marks the end of its own self-alienation.[7,22,45,105]

Now the only reason I bring all this up is that the discipline of actively passive surrender, especially under the guidance of an acknowledged spiritual master, is always being confused with childish passive dependence.[93,102] By "always" I mean, specifically, that the vast majority of orthodox psychologists and sociologists do not wish, or are not able, to tell the difference between prepersonal helplessness and dependence on a paternal authority figure, and transpersonal surrender and submission via a spiritual adept. For those scholars, apparently, the adolescent stance of active independence and fierce isolation is held to be, not a phase-specific moment in the greater arc of development, but the goal and highest stage of development itself, whereupon any stance other than that is viewed with ghoulish academic fascination.

Now, it is certainly true that many of the "new religions," or at least the new cults, are based on the dynamics of prepersonal regression/fixation, with consequent obedience to a father figure/totem master, with self-clan fusion and indissociation (participation mystique), with group ritual, magic incantations, mythic apocrypha. The members of the clan-cult often show borderline neurotic or borderline psychotic dispositions; that is, low ego-strength, concrete immersion in experience with difficulty holding abstract locations, narcissistic involvement, low self-esteem, with correlative difficulty handling moral ambiguity, contradictions, or choice structures.[4,56,59] The clan-cult is magnetic for such personalities, because it (and usually its totem master) offers and fosters an atmosphere of passive dependence to authoritarianism, which re-creates the child-specific mood in which such personalities are still psychologically trapped. Cults do not have to "brainwash" such members; all they have to do is show up and smile.

Because it caters to the child-specific mood of passive dependence, the one thing *not* allowed in the clan-cult is the exercise of active adolescent independence, especially the exercise of rational self-reflection, critical appraisal, logical discourse, and systematic study of alternative philosophies. This, coupled with the allegiance to totem master, or the magical "father" of the entire clan, constitutes much of the psychosocial foundation of the cult.

To the untutored eye, a community of transpersonal contemplatives—what the Buddhists call a *sangha*—

often appears similar or even identical to the clan-cult,

principally because, I suppose, it is usually rather close-knit and often organized around a spiritual adept held in various degrees of reverence or at least profound respect. This community is also interested in nullifying adolescent active independence, but in an entirely different direction—its transcendence, not its prohibition. In fact, because each higher stage transcends but *includes* its predecessors, the true sangha always *retains access to,* and retains an appropriate place for, rational inquiry, logical reflection, systematic study of other philosophical frameworks, and critical appraisal of its own teachings in light of related areas. Historically, in fact, the mystical centers of contemplation have often been the great centers of education and learning—Nalanda in India, for instance, or the T'ien T'ai Buddhist centers in China. Needham[64] has already demonstrated that mysticism and scientific inquiry have usually been historically linked, simply because both have always rejected dogmatic belief and insisted on open experience.

The point is that what one is attempting to "destroy" in contemplation *is not the mind but an exclusive identity of consciousness with the mind.*[101,102] The infant-child is identified more or less exclusively with the body; as the adolescent mind emerges, it destroys the exclusive identity with the body but does not destroy the body itself; it subsumes the body in its own larger mental identity. Just so, as spirit emerges, it destroys the exclusive identity with mind (and subsumed body) but does not destroy the mind itself; it subsumes the mind to its own larger supreme identity.[102] The mind itself is perfectly valued, as is its free and critical inquiry into any theoretical area.

The adolescent separate self sense, however, which is an exclusive identification with mind in a stance of fiercely macho independence, is not so highly valued; therefore, many preliminary exercises in contemplative communities are specifically designed to remind the ego

104   of its phase-specific and intermediate place in overall

development. Exercises such as simple bowing in Zen, the prostrations in Vajrayana, or mandatory community service-dharma in monastic sects, are outward and visible signs of an inward and actively passive surrender to a state of selfless being more panoramic than ego. The eventual aim of such practises is to keep the mind but transcend the egoic self sense by discovering a larger self in the spiritual dimension of creation at large.

Now, that is radically different from the clan-cult strategy of *reducing* the self to prepersonal and passive dependence by restricting and prohibiting the free engagement of critical reflection. The aim of sangha is to keep mind but transcend ego; the aim of the cult is to prohibit both.

I realize that in practise it is not always easy to determine whether a particular community is a cult or a sangha—like most life situations, there is something of a continuum between ideal limits. But I feel that the above criteria at least offer a plausible basis for the psychodynamic distinction between these groups (for an expansion of these criteria, see Wilber[106]). There is obviously much research to be done in this area, but speaking both personally and as a transpersonal psychologist, I think orthodox psychologists and sociologists could show a little more imagination when it comes to reporting on the psychodynamics of a communal occasion; they have all but made Jonestown a paradigm of "spiritual" get-togethers. I would only like to suggest that an honest effort be made to distinguish child-specific passive dependence from mature actively passive surrender, with a correlative distinction between prepersonal cults and transpersonal sanghas.

4. I have, throughout this book, been emphasizing what sociology might gain from an infusion of psychology (and transpersonal psychology in particular). I should like to emphasize, however, that this is a two-way street, and that psychology (and transpersonal psychology in

particular) has much to gain from a study of modern sociology, and especially the sociology of religions. Accordingly, I should like to end this chapter by reprinting my review of *In Gods We Trust: New Patterns of Religious Pluralism in America* (Robbins and Anthony, eds.), which was published in *Journal of Transpersonal Psychology*. That book is representative of the type of serious, disciplined, sociological inquiry that is now occurring with regard to various new religious movements in America (though we could almost say, with certain surface modifications, the Western world at large). Other such volumes are, at this moment, being compiled. No question: this is good news—for psychology, sociology, *and* religion.

My comments on this book, while not nearly as detailed as what has gone above, may nonetheless serve as a general summary of our discussion thus far, and as an indication of the type of interdisciplinary dialogue upon which the future of this field depends.

Assuming that psychology is always also social psychology, a study of the "new religions" from a decidedly sociological perspective would be of great significance to psychology in general and to transpersonal psychology/therapy in particular; even more so given the fact that a "transpersonal sociology" is a discipline desperately awaiting birth. *In Gods We Trust* is, I believe, the first rigorously sociological treatment of the new religious movements; as such, it possesses all of the strengths of a truly pioneering effort, and some of the unavoidable weaknesses; in any event, its simple appearance is monumental.

The anthology has as its starting point (and in many ways its central theme) Robert Bellah's immensely influential concept of "civil religion" and its recent disintegration. The idea, briefly, is that, whatever else the function of religion, it serves centrally as a way to meaningfully integrate and legitimate a world view [rd-2 and rd-8]. According to Bellah, American civil religion is (or was) a blend of Biblical symbolism and American nationalism ("One nation, under God. . . ."), a "religion" which adequately served social integration, ethic, and purpose for the better part of American history. However, in recent decades, according to Bellah and others, the American civil religion began to disintegrate, or, technically, to lose its legitimacy (what Bellah calls "the broken covenant"). Assuming (as these theorists do) that religion as integrative function [rd-2] is a universal necessity or impulse, it follows that *something* would have to take the place of the old civil religion; hence, the new religions of the last few decades: "The appeal of oriental mysticism and quasi-mystical therapy groups can best be understood in relation to the needs created by this decline [in civil religion]."

From that point, the anthology moves progressively into various sociological theories, research, and data, arranged in six sections. The subtitles tell the story: Religious Ferment and Cultural Transformation; Disenchantment and Renewal in Mainline Traditions; Civil Religion Sects, Oriental Mysticism and Therapy Groups; The Brainwashing Explanation (since I won't discuss this topic in the rest of this review, let me point out here that this book stands as a sound indictment of the "brainwashing" theory wherever it appears; the data simply doesn't support such an explanatory theory, even with such problematic groups as the Moonies); New Religions; and the Decline of Community. Some highlights:

Robert Wuthnow's "Political Aspects of the Quietistic Revival" is almost humorously titled (re: "quietistic"), because it effectively challenges the longstanding prejudice (found in researchers from Weber to Freud) that there is a "'hydraulic relation' between experiential religion and political commitment, that the more mystical a person is, the less involved in [social or] political activity he is likely to be." On the basis of empirical data, Wuthnow demonstrates that not only are those attracted to mysticism *not* less socially committed, they consistently ranked higher in most social commitment categories (e.g., value of social improvement, equal rights for women, solving social problems, etc.). Related is Donald Stone's "Social Consciousness in the Human Potential Movement." Based on systematically collected data, Stone suggests that at least some (not all) of the human potential movements tend to increase social responsibility by *lessening,* not increasing, narcissistic withdrawal, *contra* Lasch and other critics (although this by no means invalidates all of Lasch's arguments, which apparently do apply to some "new age" movements, the differential remaining unspecified [a differential we have suggested as pre-law versus trans-law]).

107

Robert Bellah's chapter is a clarification of his concept of "civil religion," as well as a cogent argument that, in effect, the American constitution implicitly but fatally assumed moral discipline (or purpose) would always be effected by the Church, so that, as the Church now declines, there is no obvious national moral replacement; some of the new religions then offer, not a legitimate replacement for fractured moral bonding, but a privitistic escape ("so self-centered that they begin to approximate the consumer cafeteria model").

Robbins and Anthony's own contribution includes a superb introduction—perhaps the best single chapter in the anthology; a complete and devastating critique of the brainwashing model; and an insightful report on the Meher Baba community. The latter is especially important, because it demonstrates that sophisticated sociological analysis (largely Parsonian) can be performed on a spiritual community without reductionistically denigrating the community or its teachings. (In so doing, it everywhere transcends, however subtly, strict Parsonianism.)

Finally, as a general statement, the empirical sociological data presented in the volume is both interesting and significant, demonstrating the considerable power of sociological methodology.

Because psychologists tend to study trees and not forests, and because sociologists tend to study forests and not trees, these disciplines seem always to need balancing via interdisciplinary dialogue. This seems especially true for the psychology and sociology of religion. For instance, a transpersonal psychologist might wish to point out that a few of the book's chapters contain subtle reductionistic tendencies. For example, if the "new religions" are basically the result of the disintegration of American civil religion, is that *all* they are? Is what Zen Buddhism offers *essentially* the same as what civil religion offered? Many sociologists say yes; a transpersonal psychologist would probably say no. The latter religion offered an integration of egos, the former, their transcendence—a fact that sociology as sociology tends to miss. (Although I must mention that the editors of this volume are, in their own writings, acutely attuned to this distinction.) A transpersonal psychologist might therefore acknowledge the sociological perspective by saying that the breakdown of the old civil religion was necessary but *not sufficient* for the recent interest in authentic mystical religions. *Necessary,* in that if there were no disharmony at all in orthodox religions, one would not seek elsewhere; *not sufficient,* in that the new authentically mystical traditions offer something *never* officially offered by civil or orthodox religions: actual transcendence (and not merely communal immersion).

For the same reasons, a transpersonal psychologist might point out that there seems to be a stark difference between *transpersonal* growth and *prepersonal* regression; that some of the so-called new religions or new therapies are actually prepersonal, not trans-personal; that these prepersonal movements are indeed often narcissistic, cultic, authoritarian, anti-rational, and self-centered (although via the "group self" [i.e., mythic-membership]); and these cultic movements—Jonestown, Synanon, Children of God—cannot believably be equated with authentic transpersonal sanghas, or contemplative communities—such as, perhaps, various genuine Buddhist centers (Zen, Vajrayana, Theravadin), Christian mystical enclaves, some Yoga centers, etc. But again, sociology *as* sociology [or functionalism bereft of hierarchic structuralism] tends to miss these types of distinctions, since it sees only what these forests have in common: they are all different from mainstream, orthodox religions.

But if those are the types of things sociology might learn from transpersonal psychology, *In Gods We Trust* is an extraordinary compendium of what transpersonal psychologists can learn from modern sociology. I mean explicitly to include psychologists in general, but transpersonal psychologists and therapists in particular. For, as we said, if such theories are not sufficient for transpersonalists, they nevertheless remain absolutely necessary. Just as psychoanalysis of productions "on the couch" can't tell you about the sanity of society at large, so the study of the productions "on the zazen mat" can't tell you about larger and equally significant societal currents. In my opinion, many of the recalcitrant theoretical problems faced by transpersonal psychology have already been substantially answered by the sociology of religion, and *In Gods We Trust* is exactly a compendium of such answers.

This anthology is all the more significant given the commitment of its editors. Dick Anthony, for instance, is acutely aware of the difference between regressive, prepersonal, and pre-rational movements and progressive, transpersonal, and trans-rational concerns. His work is permeated with a genuine sensitivity to non-reductionistic interpretations of spiritual endeavors. Moreover, he is, in conjunction with Jacob Needle-

109

man, Thomas Robbins, and others, almost singlehandedly initiating the dialogue between orthodox sociologists and transpersonal psychologists. *In Gods We Trust* is not that dialogue—it is (and was appropriately intended to be) a genuinely sociological anthology, with little psychology, transpersonal or otherwise. But beyond that stated aim, which it thoroughly achieves, it is an invitation to a future dialogue with transpersonal psychologists, an invitation whose significance cannot be overestimated, and an invitation to which I trust psychologists in general, and transpersonal psychologists in particular, will enthusiastically respond.

8

KNOWLEDGE AND HUMAN INTERESTS

In this chapter I would like to take Habermas's work on knowledge and cognitive interests as a starting base for extending sociology, and especially a critical sociology, into a more truly comprehensive formulation, one capable of adequately embracing authentically spiritual or actually transcendental *knowledge* and *interest*. Since I wish only to suggest certain possibilities, the discussion will be conducted on a more than usually generalized and preliminary level.

Habermas[38] distinguishes three principal modes of knowledge-inquiry: the empirical-analytic, which deals with objectifiable processes; the historical-hermeneutic, which aims at interpretive understanding of symbolic configurations; and the critical-reflective, which apprehends (past) cognitive operations and thus subjects them to a measure of insight.

The especially intriguing part of Habermas's theory is that each mode is intrinsically linked to a type of human *interest,* for knowledge as knowledge is always moved and moving. To get an idea of what Habermas means by cognitive interests, if every time you wanted to know something you asked yourself, "*Why* do I want to know this?" and then removed all the purely personal-idiosyncratic motives, you would have the *general cog-*

nitive interest that guides the particular process of inquiry.

According to Habermas,[38] "The approach of the empirical-analytic sciences incorporates a *technical* cognitive interest; that of the historic-hermeneutic sciences incorporates a *practical* one; and the approach of critically oriented sciences incorporates the *emancipatory* cognitive interest." *Technical* interest is interest in predicting and controlling events in the objectifiable environment. *Practical* interest is interest in understanding and sharing the mutualities of life, morality, purpose, goals, values, and such. *Emancipatory* interest is interest in releasing the distortions and constraints of labor, language, or communication that result from their nontransparency, or their not being looked at steadily with critical awareness. (At this point, I remind the reader that we have earlier distinguished between horizontal emancipation, which aims at redressing the distortions within any given level, and vertical emancipation, which aims at moving to a higher level altogether. Habermas treats only the former, and therefore I will always refer to his as horizontal-emancipatory interest.)

I am now going to take two shortcuts. First, I am going to use only our three general domains of the sub, self, and superconscient, by the names of physical-sensorimotor, mental-rational, and spiritual-transcendental, or body, mind, and spirit for short. Body possesses a degree of *pre-*symbolic or sensory knowledge; mind works with symbolic knowledge; and spirit deals with *trans-*symbolic knowledge or gnosis. Notice that mind, being *the* symbolic mode, can form symbols *of* each of the three domains: the material world, the mental world itself, and the spiritual world. Those three modes of symbolic knowledge, when added to trans-symbolic gnosis and pre-symbolic awareness, give us five general modes of cognition. Figure 4 indicates these modes.

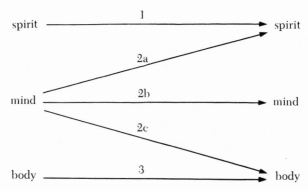

Figure 4
Five General Modes of Cognition

Number 1 is spiritual gnosis, or spirit's direct and non-mediated knowledge *of* spirit *as* spirit. Number 2a is what has been called paradoxical or mandalic reason, because it is mind's attempt to put into mental symbols that which is finally trans-mental, and the result is always eventually paradoxical. Number 2b is mind's knowledge of other minds, or a symbol's awareness of other symbols, as when you are reading this. Number 2c is the mind's awareness of the physical and sensory world, or the symbol-models used to picture the *pre-* symbolic world. Number 3 is the sensorimotor apprehension of the sensorimotor world, or the pre-symbolic grasp of the pre-symbolic world.

In my opinion, those forms of knowledge are *grounded* in the levels of *structural organization* themselves. The deep structures of developmental or self-forming consciousness dictate the very *forms* of those cognitions; to that extent they are invariant, deep-rooted, native, and collective (although, of course, their surface structures are in large measure culturally molded and conditioned).

My second shortcut is to identify Habermas's empirical-analytic mode with number 2c, or mind's awareness of the empirical-sensory world; and his historical-hermeneutic mode with number 2b, or mind's
113   interaction with other minds. This is a shortcut because

the distinctions are not precise; for example, insofar as a hermeneutic occasion has an empirically objective component, that component can become object to empirical-analytic inquiry; likewise, insofar as a sensory-objective occasion comes under interpretive understanding, it can become object to historical-hermeneutic inquiry. Nonetheless, it is my opinion that the central form, the very paradigm, of empirical-analytic inquiry is symbolic mind reflecting pre-symbolic world, and the paradigm of historical-hermeneutic inquiry is symbolic mind interacting with symbolic mind. To put it crudely, the former is mind reflecting matter; the latter, mind reflecting mind. As a generalization, then, we use number 2b as historical-hermeneutic and number 2c as empirical-analytic, and we assign them their respective cognitive interests, practical-moral and technical-predictive, which are all listed in Figure 5.

What, then, are we to make of Habermas's horizontal-emancipatory interest, the interest in "clearing up" the distortions in relational exchange on each major level? If knowledge and human interests are really grounded in *structures*, we should be able to point to a central structure as paradigmatic for this emancipatory interest (as we pointed to number 2c for empirical-technical, etc.). And yet, for reasons that will become clearer as we proceed, none of the five cognitive modes quite fits the bill. For one thing, horizontal-emancipatory interest apparently can operate on all or almost all levels. For another, it is not *necessarily* operative, but comes into existence only if there have, in fact, been distortions that demand clarification. As Habermas[38] puts it,

Compared with the technical and practical interests in knowledge, which are both grounded in deeply rooted (invariant? [i.e., deep?]) structures of action and experience . . . , the [horizontal-] *emancipatory interest in knowledge* has a derivative status. It guarantees the connection between theoretical knowledge and an "object domain" of practical life which comes into existence as a result of systematically distorted communication and thinly legitimated repression.

The horizontal-emancipatory interest, in other words, is rooted not so much in specific structures per se, for it then would be continually active, but rather in structural *tension* caused by structural distortion, and its aim is to remove the source of the tension. Once the distortions are gone, the horizontal-emancipatory interest loses its juice. It is therefore not surprising that the only two major instances of such horizontal-emancipatory concerns given by Habermas (other than his own work) are Freudian psychoanalysis and Marxist materialist critique.

To put it simplistically, the need for psychoanalysis arises only when something "goes wrong" in psychological development. Psychological distortions—repressions and oppressions—give rise to psychological tensions; these tensions can be resolved only by a critical reflection on, or analysis of, "what went wrong" itself, and this critical-reflective knowledge has as its *interest* the *emancipation* from those distortions, obstructions, and repressions. Marxist material-economic critique operates in a similar fashion—past (historical) economic oppressions give rise to societal tensions. These tensions (class struggle, false consciousness, alienated labor, opaque ideology) can be resolved only by a critical analysis of their historical (developmental) genesis, with an interest in the emancipation from such oppressive economic distortions. And what Habermas himself is doing, with his philosophy of communicative ethics, is using critical-reflective inquiry and horizontal-emancipatory interest in an attempt to illumine and then correct the distortions and restraints placed upon what should otherwise be free and open *communicative exchange*. The oppression of communication and intersubjective exchange gives rise to distortions in discourse (and truth) itself—propaganda being the simplest example. Such "systematically distorted communication and thinly legit-

115

imated repression" generates both the possibility and the necessity for critical-reflective inquiry into such distortions with an interest in the emancipation from such opaque communication. *In all three cases,* once the distortions are cleared, the need for analysis and the interest in emancipation both tend to wane, since they have served their purpose by dissolving their own source.

I would simply add that, in my opinion, the fact that Freud and Marx were both aware of the importance of communicative exchange in their various fields should not conceal the fact that material-economic obstruction (which most but not solely interested Marx), and emotional-sexual obstruction (which most but not solely interested Freud), and communicative obstruction (which most but not solely interests Habermas) refer to quite different structural levels of relational exchange and potential distortion. *The horizontal-emancipatory interest can swing into play with regard to each,* but the actual dynamics are slightly different in each case because the object domain of each has a different structure. To put it simply, "clearing up" matter, clearing up sex, and clearing up communication are all forms of horizontal-emancipation, but the concrete dynamics differ in each case because the dynamics of matter, emotions, and thoughts are themselves different. After all, the murder of Socrates, for example, was not a result of economic-material distortion nor emotional-sexual repression, but communicative oppression. These various distortions, like the levels they infect, are hierarchic. And in that hierarchy of disease, what Marx did *primarily* for the material sphere, and Freud did *primarily* for the emotional sphere, Habermas is now doing primarily for the communicative (mental) sphere. Those three theorists stand as exemplars of the horizontal-emancipatory interest on those levels. (We are still awaiting the analyst who as brilliantly studies the distortions and oppressions of spirituality, the repression of transcendence, the politics of Tao, the denial of Being by beings.)

We can now fill out Figure 5 by adding the other forms of knowledge and their respective interests. I tentatively suggest the following: the interest of mode number 3, or bodily knowledge of the sensory world, is *instinctual;* the schemata of sensorimotor cognition are grounded in instinctual survival. The interest of mode number 2a, or the mind's attempt to reason about spirit, is *soteriological*— interest in salvation; an attempt to comprehend spirit in mental terms so as either to orient oneself toward the pull of a transcendental intuition or to help "picture" the spiritual realm for those minds not yet so *interested.* (The picture is always eventually paradoxical, as both Kant and Nagarjuna explained, but this neither hampers the human interest in the divine nor restricts the usefulness of mandalic reason; e.g., there is some sort of useful information carried in the paradoxical-mandalic statement that spirit is both perfectly transcendent and perfectly immanent.) The interest of gnosis, mode number 1, or spirit's knowledge of spirit as spirit, is *liberational*— interest in radical liberation (satori, moksha, wu, release). Where soteriological interest wishes to present to the self a higher knowledge, liberational interest aims at dissolving the self into higher knowledge *as* that knowledge, that is, as spirit's knowledge of and as spirit. The former wishes, as self, to be saved by spirit; the latter wishes, as spirit, to transcend self.

It remains to comment on the vertical-emancipatory interest. Like its cousin the horizontal-emancipatory interest, it is generated not so much by a specific structure as by a structural *tension,* and its interest is to remove the source of the tension. But here the source is not a tension *within* a particular level but a tension *between* levels; specifically, the tension of *emergence,* the tension of a coming transformation, or vertical shift in levels of structural organization. The aim of this vertical-emancipatory interest is to free awareness, not from a distortion that might or might not happen within a level, but from the relatively limited perspective offered by that level even at

117

its best—and to do so by opening awareness to the next higher level of structural organization. This interest cannot be allayed by clearing up the distortions within a level but only by the emergence of the next higher level. We may suppose that the interest then temporarily wanes, until (and if) the inherent limitations of the next level begin increasingly to display themselves, and emancipation *from,* not *within,* that level increasingly exerts itself. Barring arrest, such vertical-emancipatory interest will continue periodically until final emancipation, that is, until satori. At that point, the last form of vertical-emancipatory interest coincides precisely with liberational interest; that is, the two are the same at the asymptotic limit of growth. All in all, the interest of horizontal-emancipation is to clear up translation; the interest of vertical-emancipation is to promote transformation.

Figure 5 lists all of these modes of knowledge and their interests.

My point, then, introductory as it may be, is that when we add these various modes and interests of human knowledge to the various levels of structural organization and relational exchange of the human compound individual, with all the corollaries and psychosocial displays suggested in the other chapters, we have the outlines of a fairly comprehensive (though far from completed) sociological theory: a skeleton, as it were. We have most of the bones here, even if we do not know yet everything to hang on them. But at least we make perfect and appropriate room for the prepersonal, the personal, and the transpersonal dimensions of existence—their levels, their development, their social exchange nature, their possible repressive (psychological) and oppressive (social) distortions, their modes of knowing and interest, their structural organization, their functional relations. And it is a truly *critical* and *normative* sociological theory, by virtue

of the two emancipatory interests that rear their heads

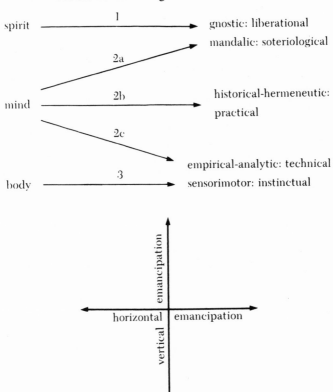

Figure 5

Modes of Knowledge and Their Interests

wherever structural nonfreedom and nontransparency arise. This critical (what went wrong) and normative (what should go right) dimension, especially in its vertical form, is not based *on* ideological preference, dogmatic inclination, or theoretical conjecture, but *in* the observable, verifiable, inherently preferred direction of structural development and evolution, a direction that discloses itself in successive hierarchic emancipations that *themselves* pass judgments on their less transcendental predecessors.

9

METHODOLOGY, SUMMARY, AND CONCLUSION

I WOULD like to summarize and conclude this outline by giving an example of proposed methodology in a sociological investigation of a religious group, with specific emphasis on any psychotherapeutic counseling that might be requested (not that such therapy is necessary, but the topic always seems to come up with regard to "religious groups," and so I will take the opportunity to comment in general). This will be merely a specialized example of the overall sociological methodology implicit in the model we have presented throughout this book.

A. Structural Analysis (Determination of Authenticity)

1. Whenever sociologists are met with an apparently religious expression, they may, in addition to other methodological approaches (described below), perform a *structural* analysis on the *form* of the expressions, symbologies, psychosocial exchanges, and so forth. The aim of such standard structural analysis is, by means of in-

121

creasingly subtracting/abstracting the surface structures, to arrive at the deep structure underlying and governing the operations (i.e., translations) of the surface structures themselves.[5,70,101] This analysis aims, in effect, to assign all surface structures to their appropriate deep structure by demonstrating that they obey the transcriptive rules of the particular deep structure (or that they can, via transcription, be resolved into the deep structure).

Such structural analyses might include any of the tests devised by, for example, Kohlberg; Loevinger; Broughton; Sullivan, Grant, and Grant; Isaacs; Peck; Bull; Selman; and Graves. That these various formulations are all *roughly* correlative has been demonstrated by Loevinger;[57] in any event, they suffice perfectly to give us a first approximation of the degree of general structural organization reached by the central belief systems embraced by the group. We are not so much interested in the scores of any *particular* members, although those can certainly be ascertained (and should be ascertained for any member specifically seeking counseling). Rather, we wish structurally to analyze the central belief systems by which the group *defines itself.* One way of determining this is to structurally analyze the occasion that *defines membership in the group;* that is, What interaction, series of interactions, or belief structures must be internalized by a person in order to be socially *recognized* as a member of this group? What has to be "in" a person before the person is officially "in" the group? What level of "food" has to be digested by initiates in order to be "family"? For it is *that* occasion, embodying *that* mana, which marks the central-level or base-level of structural organization by which the group defines its self-identity and around which the group as group inevitably revolves. If there are levels of initiation/belief, analysis is applied at each level. (As for structural tests for the higher-authentic levels, see below, section A, 3.)

2. Once an approximate determination of central-level deep structure has been made, its relative location on the developmental hierarchy of structuralization can be determined. For example, is this "religious involvement" archaic, magical, mythical, rational, psychic, subtle, causal? (Or, for example, Loevinger: symbiotic, impulsive, self-protective, conformist, conscientious, individualistic, autonomous, integrated? and so on.)

This determination—or something like it—is especially important for counseling purposes, because in psychotherapeutic service (and social work) it is a great advantage, as psychoanalytic ego psychology has clearly demonstrated, to know the degree of structuralization reached by the self-system in question.[17] Are there archaic fusion elements (self-group indissociation, archaic-uroboric "oneness," oral-cannibalistic trends)? Is there borderline structure present (magical-psychotic, animistic, totem confusion, delusional reference systems)? Is there extreme mythic-membership conformity (with terror of individuality, surrender of self-will and determination, yearning for belongingness and cultic association, passive dependence on authority figures)? Is there rational structure but with possible complicating side-issues (merely and more or less healthy counter-law tendencies, or actual neurotic splitting, symptomology, and identity crisis)? Is there actual psychic, subtle, or causal structure, but with consequent alienation from mainstream mythic or rational consensus (communication viscosity, social isolation, possible depression)?

I cannot emphasize too strongly the importance of such structural diagnosis; without it, any therapeutic intervention can be disastrous.[102] As only a simple example, take the differences between pre-rational and trans-rational engagements. A pre-rational, borderline individual, who needs desperately to create rational structure and ego strength, should not be introduced to the more strenuous trans-rational meditative-yogic disciplines, because they are designed to *loosen* the rational structure temporarily and thus will simply dismantle what little structure the borderline has left. Likewise, such clients, in my opinion, should not be exposed to "experiential" therapies, since they already live too much in the experience and not enough in the mind.[17] Conversely, someone beginning or undergoing a true transformation to psychic-subtle realms will find no help from an orthodox psychiatrist, who tends to see all trans-rational development as pre-rational regression, and who, in helping to re-entrench exclusive rational structure in this person, will deliver his spiritual consciousness stillborn. Such a person should be referred to a qualified spiritual master, Jungian therapist, a transpersonal psychologist, or some other authentically oriented service.

In short, the aim of structural analysis is to determine the *type,* and consequently the *degree,* of developmental structuralization and organization, and correlatively, if the situation claims religiosity, its degree of authenticity.

3. The above analysis, of course, will eventually hinge on a more refined developmental-structural hierarchy than we have presented here. The refinement and sophistication of this hierarchy will occur through the continued structural-developmental-stage research in psychological cognition, identity, perception, moralization, natural epistemology, and so on. This refinement is already occurring—has been occurring for quite some time—on the subconscient and self-conscient realms of structuralization, under the names of psychoanalytic developmental psychology, cognitive psychology, genetic epistemology, developmental ego psychology, and so on. As interest and research increasingly extend to the superconscient realms, we will naturally (I

assume) witness a refinement-sophistication of the developmental-structural hierarchies with regard to the higher and contemplative levels. The initial phases of this research seem likely to follow two stages.

a. *Hermeneutical reading of authentic texts:* In order to map out research design and strategy, it is necessary to have some sort of working hypotheses, and one of the best sources of such working sets seems to be the experimental-maps of superconscious stages offered by the traditional texts. A careful and systematic hermeneutical reading of the various (esoteric) religious texts will help provide us with a fund of working hypotheses-maps around which to frame actual research and against which to judge initial progress. *The Atman Project* is a basic but very general attempt in this direction, drawing on *cross-cultural parallels* to suggest some basic deep structures of the higher stage-levels (centauric, low-subtle, high-subtle, low-causal, high-causal, and ultimate, which I have condensed in this book to psychic, subtle, causal, and ultimate). Daniel Brown[20] has presented a hermeneutical reading of one particular stage-conception of higher meditative states, that of Mahamudra, which is the type of detailed hermeneutics we will need in each esoteric tradition so that we can draw more precisely our cross-cultural parallels and conclusions. The works of Pascal Kaplan,[55] Daniel Goleman,[35] Huston Smith,[86] Fritjof Schuon,[81] and René Guénon[37] are important guides in this endeavor.

b. *Direct investigation:* In order to test our refined hypothetical maps, we will need actual data accumulation from populations of those genuinely engaged in superconscient development and adaptation. This topic itself demands no less than book-length treatment, and instead of even trying to mention all the pertinent points (and problems), I will only say that, using the hermeneutical working maps, we will be able to design proposed characterologies of the higher structure-stages, construct adequate tests to register and measure the emergence and degree of these traits, and eventually subject the results to standard structural analyses à la Piaget, Kohlberg, Loevinger, and others. These will be repeated wherever possible in cross-cultural conditions (Japan, India, Burma, etc., have very large contemplative sectors, as does now the United States). Initial work is being done in this area by Maliszewski, Twemlow, Brown, Engler, Gabbard, Jones, and others.[21,58,92]

I feel this field is especially ripe for sociologists, since almost all research to date has overlooked the intersubjective patterns of relational exchange that constitute the higher as well as lower levels of structural adaptation. Psychologists interested only in perceptual changes, cognitive shifts, affect reinterpretation, impulse control, and such meditators tend to overlook the psycho*social* nature of their artificially isolated data, just as psychoanalysts tended to overlook the fact that analysis of productions "on the couch" cannot tell you that the society at large might itself be sick, and adaptation to a sick society is a poor criterion of "mental health." Just as analysis of social patterns at large cannot be conducted on the couch, so identification of the fundamental psychosocial relationships constitutive of the contemplative realms cannot be conducted on the zazen mat. Transpersonal psychology will eventually have to find itself in transpersonal sociology.

As for the direct investigation of the superconscient realms, as opposed to indirect psychological or sociological data accumulation, see below, section E.

B. Functional Analysis (Determination of Legitimacy)

1. Once the degree of authenticity of the religious expression is determined via structural analysis, the de-

gree of legitimacy can be determined via standard functionalist (systems theory) approaches. The point is simply to determine how well the particular religious engagement is serving stability and integration *within* the group itself (content legitimacy) and *between* the group and its broader societal background (context legitimacy). Here all the standard functional analyses and more or less empirical-analytic determinations swing into play—tension management, pattern maintenance, boundary determinations, content and context analyses, latent and manifest functions, and so forth[62,69]—but with a refined understanding as to hierarchic levels of structural interaction. For example, if the particular group is determined (via previous structural analysis) to be pre-law, that fact will set a boundary with relation to law that is not merely between two systems but between two different levels of systems, a fact that functionalism itself cannot detect (lacking normative hierarchy). We have to use developmental structuralism to impose this boundary condition, or else the functional analyses tend to slide over (and then collapse into) each other.

With regard to legitimacy/illegitimacy, here are what seem to be some common content and context patterns. Frequently, pre-law sectors (or individuals) are found to be both content *and* context illegitimate, which means that their symbologies and relational exchanges provide little or no internal mana/integration and little or no larger societal co-existence (in which case they are always on the verge of anti-law engagement). However, it is not uncommon to find content and context legitimate pre-law sectors (e.g., stereotypical gypsies, although in America they are supposedly always on the verge of context illegitimacy, i.e., anti-law) or "part-time" pre-law sectors (i.e., serve societal law-translations "by day" and benign but ritual pre-law celebrations "by night," e.g., witches covens). Perhaps most common, however, are pre-law groups that no matter how possibly content legitimate are context illegitimate (i.e., anti-law; e.g., Hell's Angels).

At the other end of the spectrum, it is not uncommon to find an *authentic* religious expression that is having context legitimation difficulties *because* it is trans-law. Such trans-laws therefore, for functional pattern maintenance and tension management, tend to form micro-communities of like-minded practitioners (sanghas), which is simply another way of saying that, since each level of structural adaptation *is* a level of relational exchange, communities of exchange partners are inevitable, and it is within that community that one measure of legitimation is sought (content legitimation). But also we want to watch the boundary phenomena *between* trans-law groups and the law-society at large (context legitimation), and, for particular individuals, how they handle (integrate) the structural tensions of living in both sectors.

2. All in all, then, the overall patterns of social interrelation seem to be determined in part by (a) the degree of authenticity and (b) the degree of legitimacy, evidenced (c) within and (d) across each boundary situation. Thus, the *internal content* of a given group will be among the set: (pre-law, counter-law, law, anti-law, trans-law) X (legitimate, illegitimate). Likewise, *between* each group and its larger societal background (context) there are the same ten possibilities (although one of them—anti-law context legitimacy—is for all practical purposes an impossibility). The overall result is a display of twenty (or nineteen) different possible cells into which any psychosocial exchange in general, and any religious expression in particular, will fall.

Now by no means am I implying that that analysis is complete or even adequate, and I certainly do not wish to exclude other typologies. My only point is that by adding a basic structural-hierarchical analysis to the standard functional ones, we achieve a vertical (authenticity) scale in addition to a horizontal (legitimacy) scale, and it is this combination that gives us four compass points by which to navigate our sociological investigations.

C. The Hermeneutical Moment

1. If the structural and functional analyses form the methodological backbone of this approach, they by no means exhaust the necessary approaches. Deep structural analysis *cannot* determine specific surface structure contents and values, just as the rules of chess cannot tell you which moves a particular player will actually make. Nor is overall functionalism helpful here, because it sees forests and not trees. So, for specific understandings of specific individual values, meanings, and expressions, we always rely on phenomenological-hermeneutics. In this task we are helped by our prior structural and functional analyses, for they provide, respectively, the proper narrative foil (i.e., developmental hierarchy) and proper narrative context (i.e., the relation of the individual text to society at large). But in the last analysis, we are face to face with a living person who reads us while we read him or her, and this co-production is a human sharing in which both sides are correspondingly enriched or diminished.

For this general phenomenological-hermeneutics, we have the important works of, for example, Gadamer, Schutz, Berger and Luckmann, Garfinkle, Taylor, Ricoeur.

2. For specific therapeutic service, the hermeneutic procedure involves a conscious *interpretation* of symptoms deemed problematic by the client, with the eventual aim of re-constructing the possible developmental miscarriages that splintered or fragmented the ongoing sweep of structuralization. When this fragmentation occurs, aspects of consciousness are split off and thus become opaque in their meaning. They are "hidden texts," alienated facets of self, dissociated *symbols* that show up as *symptoms*. By *interpreting* the symbol-symptoms—the hidden texts and subtexts—the therapist helps the client to re-own those facets of self by *re-authoring* them and

129

thus re-authorizing them, that is consciously assuming responsibility for their existence.[105]

This is where a general knowledge of development as ongoing hierarchical structuralization is so essential, because the historical-hermeneutic procedure is not merely digging into past developments on the present level, but into past and *less structured* levels, whose meanings are very difficult to *translate* without a knowledge of past *transformations*. The therapist, for instance, might find that, within the client's rational, linguistic, conscious communication of a particular message or series of messages, there is a hidden meaning, a subtext. Now this opaque subtext might indeed be a fairly rational message itself, but one the client wishes not to acknowledge (taboo for the moment); therapy here involves not much more than the therapist's providing a *context* for the acknowledgment of the rational subtext. However, on occasion the hidden message, the opaque communication, the subtext, is written in *mythic* syntax, which itself might have a core of *magical* wish-fulfillments (which *in turn* are often informed or subtexted by archaic *instinctual* or emotional-sexual interests).[35, 101, 105]

In such cases, apparently, at some point in the course of early development, a magical (and/or emotional) subtext was deemed taboo and defensively split off (repressed, dissociated) from the ongoing march of structuralization. Since structures are always structures *of* relational exchange, this also involves a *privitization* of what otherwise could form a unit in intersubjective exchange. That is, the alienation from self *is* an alienation from others. Once cut off from personal understanding and removed likewise from all possibility of consensual interpretation, it becomes an illegitimate subtext isolated from the narrative of ongoing development. Thus alienated from immediate narration, isolated and privitized, it tends to draw around itself any other subsequently outlawed elements. Thus gathering layer after layer of *mis-*

translation (distorted relational exchange), it finally protrudes into awareness as a baffling symptom. And baffling it is, because, as a doubly secret text, hidden to both self and others, it has no referent for interpretation; it remains clothed in opaque symbols and nontransparent urges. Ask the client why he or she is producing such symptoms or what they mean, and the client replies, "I have no idea; that's why I'm here. Why is this happening? Why won't it stop?" The very fact that the client usually refers to a symptom as "it," instead of "I" or "me," (e.g., "*I* move my hand, but the symptom, *it* happens against my will") mirrors exactly the dissociated, alienated, and foreign state into which the now hidden impulse or subtext or shadow-message has fallen. Indeed, when Freud summarized the goal of therapy as "Where it was, there I shall become" (poorly translated from the original as "Where id was, there ego shall be"), he must have had essentially this crucial point in mind.

Part of the therapeutic procedure, therefore, is to use this knowledge of structural development (archaic to magic to mythic to rational) as a narrative foil against which to interpret the hidden meanings of the various subtexts, until those meanings once again become transparent to the client (i.e., nonrepressed). At that point, the symptom tends to wane because its symbolic content has been released from its privitized alienation to rejoin the community of relational exchange, and its bioenergetic component (should it have one) is released for bodily participation in emotional-sexual sharing, and its overall meaning-message has rejoined the individual's ongoing narrative unfoldment. In this overall procedure, developmental structuralism gives us the external narrative foil, and hermeneutics gives us the various internal-personal meanings of the various subtexts as they unfold against (and because of) the narrative foil itself.

3. There is, as we mentioned earlier, the role of hermeneutics in suggesting initial working maps of the

higher realms (via textual analysis of the world's esoteric traditions). Here I would only like to issue a caveat: as researchers such as Brown have suggested, a hermeneutic reading of esoteric texts discloses hierarchic stages of contemplative development. It is important to remember, however, that the hierarchy or stage-conception itself is *not* a hermeneutical disclosure. The stages are disclosed via developmental-logic—the narrative foil—in actual practise and evolution. These successive *emergent* occasions everywhere surprise narrative; however, when the overall results are simply entered in a text, it may deceptively appear that they are created by the text and therefore discoverable solely by hermeneutics, which is not the whole case, as I tried to suggest in Chapter 1, C.

D. Emancipatory Moments

Without laboring the point, I will take it as obvious that overall therapy involves a critical self-reflection on past translations and possible mistranslations (hidden texts). I believe this is true for individuals as well as for societies at large (although obviously the specifics vary). Such reflection is driven by the *horizontal-emancipatory interest*—a desire to "clear up" past mistranslations (hidden subtexts, repressions, oppressions, dissociations). These distortions, secretly lodged in the hierarchy of the compound individual, generate structural tensions and irritations that drive the emancipatory interest. When such fixations/repressions are re-membered, re-authored, and re-integrated, then those aspects of individual consciousness (or groups of people) formerly trapped in a lower level of structuralization become liberated, or capable of transformation-upward, thus surrendering their symptomatic complaints and rejoining the average higher mode of structuralization now characteristic of the central self (or society at large). Such transformative advance is driven by the *vertical-emancipatory interest* inherent in development and evolution itself.

E. The Methodology of Direct Gnostic Verification

There is, finally, the methodological problem of the *direct* (as opposed to textual) investigation of the higher (superconscient) levels themselves, and here we draw on our last two major modes of inquiry: gnosis/jnana for direct apprehension of these levels, and mandalic-logic to communicate them, however paradoxically, in linguistic symbols. For spiritual knowledge itself is *not* symbolic; it involves direct, nonmediated, trans-symbolic intuition of and identity with spirit.[7,22,88] As I have tried to suggest elsewhere,[99] this spiritual knowledge, *like all other forms of valid cognitive knowledge,* is experimental, repeatable, and publicly verifiable, because, like all other valid modes, it consists of three strands:

1. *Injunction:* always of the form, "If you want to know this, *do* this."
2. *Apprehension:* a cognitive apprehension-illumination of the "object domain" addressed by the injunction.
3. *Communal confirmation:* a checking of results with others who have adequately completed the injunctive and illuminative strands.

I shall give an example of all three strands in, say, empirical-analytic sciences. If you want to know whether a cell really contains a nucleus, then you must (1) learn to operate a microscope, learn to take histological sections, learn to stain cells, and so forth (injunctions), then (2) look and see (apprehension), then (3) compare your apprehensions with those of others, especially a qualified teacher if you are just beginning, or a community of like-minded scientific adepts if you are professionally continuing a career (communal confirmation).

Bad injunctive theories (No. 1) will be rebuffed by noncongruent apprehensions (No. 2) and subsequently rejected by the community of investigators (No. 3), and it is this potential rebuff that constitutes the non-verifiability principle of Popper.

Just so with authentic spiritual knowledge. For example, we will take Zen, vis-à-vis the three strands. It has an injunctive strand, which requires years of specialized training and critical discipline: the practise of meditation, or zazen, which is the injunctive tool for possible cognitive disclosure. Not surprisingly, then, it is always of the form "If you want to know whether there is Buddha-nature, you must first do this." That is *experimental* and *experiential* injunction.

After that strand is mastered, the investigator is opened to the second strand, that of apprehension-illumination; in this case, satori. Satori is a "direct seeing into one's nature"—as perfectly direct as looking into the microscope to see the cell nucleus, with the important proviso in each case: only a trained eye need look.

The third strand is careful confirmation, by both a Zen Master and the community of participant meditators. This is no merely automatic pat on the back and mutual-agreement society; it is a vigorous *test,* and it constitutes a potentially powerful rebuff and *nonverification* of any particular apprehension suffered in strand number 2. Both in private, intense interaction with the Zen Master (dokusan) and in exacting public participation in rigorous tests of authenticity (shosan), *all* apprehensions are struck against the community of those whose cognitive eyes are adequate to the transcendent, and such apprehensions are soundly nonverified if they do not match the facts of transcendence as disclosed by the community of like-spirited (and this includes past apprehensions once judged, by the standards of the times, to be true but now subrated or found to be partial by more sophisticated experience).[99]

It is with gnosis, then, verifiable gnosis, that our methodological repertoire is completed. And it is with gnosis that I end my informal sketch of a transpersonal sociology. For the final contribution that transpersonal psychology can make to sociology is, if you want to know about the actually transcendent realms themselves, then take up a contemplative-meditative practise (injunction) and find out for yourself (illumination), at which point the all-inclusive community of transcendence may disclose itself in your case and be tested in the fire of the like-spirited (confirmation). At that point, God ceases to be a mere symbol in your awareness but becomes the crowning level of your own compound individuality and structural adaptation, the society of all possible societies, which you now recognize as your own true self. And when God is thus seen as the society of all possible societies, the study of sociology takes on a new and unexpected meaning, and we all find ourselves immersed in a sociable God, formed and forming, liberated and liberating—a God that, as Other, demands participation, and that, as Self, demands identity.

REFERENCES

The following is by no means a comprehensive or even representative bibliography. It is merely a list of those works directly mentioned or quoted in the text. I have included a short list of recommended reading in transpersonal psychology for those who might be unfamiliar with its basic tenets.

1. Anonymous. *Course in miracles*. 3 vols. New York: Foundation for Inner Peace, 1977.
2. Anthony, D. "A phenomenological-structuralist approach to the scientific study of religion." chap. 8, *On religion and social science*. D. Anthony *et al.*, eds., University of California, forthcoming.
3. Anthony, D., and Robbins, T. "From symbolic realism to structuralism." *Journ. Sc. Study Rel.,* vol. 14, no. 4, 1975.
4. Anthony, D., and Robbins, T. "A typology of non-traditional religions in modern America." Paper, A.A.A.S., 1977.
5. Arieti, S. *The intra-psychic self*. New York: Basic Books, 1967.
6. Assagioli, R. *Psychosynthesis*. New York: Viking, 1965.
7. Aurobindo. *The life divine, and the synthesis of yoga*. vols. 18–21, Pondicherry: Centenary Library, n.d.
8. Baldwin, J. *Thought and things*. New York: Arno, 1975.
9. Bateson, G. *Steps to an ecology of mind*. New York: Ballantine, 1972.
10. Becker, E. *The denial of death*. New York: Free Press, 1973.
11. ————. *Escape from evil*. New York: Free Press, 1975.
12. Bell, D. *The end of ideology*. Glencoe: Free Press, 1960.
13. Bellah, R. *Beyond belief*. New York: Harper, 1970.
14. ————. *The broken covenant*. New York: Seabury, 1975.

15. Berdyaev, N. *The destiny of man*. New York: Harper, 1960.
16. Berger, P., and Luckmann, T. *The social construction of reality*. New York: Doubleday, 1972.
17. Blanck, G., and Blanck, R. *Ego psychology: theory and practice*. New York: Columbia Univ. Press, 1974.
18. Broughton, J. "The development of natural epistemology in adolescence and early adulthood." Doctoral dissertation, Harvard, 1975.
19. Brown, N. *Life against death*. Middletown: Wesleyan, 1959.
20. Brown, D., "A model for the levels of concentrative meditation." *Int. J. Clin. Exp. Hypnosis,* vol. 25, 1977.
21. Brown, D. and Engler, J. "A Rorschach study of the stages of mindfulness meditation." *J. Transp. Psych.,* 1980.
22. Bubba (Da) Free John. *The paradox of instruction*. San Francisco: Dawn Horse, 1977.
23. Campbell, J. *The masks of god: primitive mythology*. New York: Viking, 1959.
24. Chomsky, N. *Problems of knowledge and freedom*. London: Barrie and Jenkins, 1972.
25. Clark, G., and Piggott, S. *Prehistoric societies*. New York: Knopf, 1965.
26. Deutsch, E. *Advaita vedanta*. Honolulu: East-West Center Press, 1969.
27. Eliade, M. *Shamanism*. New York: Pantheon, 1964.
28. Fairbairn, W. *An object-relations theory of the personality*. New York: Basic Books, 1954.
29. Fenichel, O. *The psychoanalytic theory of neurosis*. New York: Norton, 1945.
30. Fenn, R. "Towards a new sociology of religion." *J. Sc. Study Rel.,* vol. 11, no. 1, 1972.
31. Freud, S. *The future of an illusion*. New York: Norton, 1971.
32. Gadamer, H. *Philosophical hermeneutics*. Berkeley: Univ. Cal. Press, 1976.
33. Garfinkel, H. *Studies in ethnomethodology*. Englewood Cliffs: Prentice-Hall, 1967.
34. Geertz, C. *The interpretation of cultures*. New York: Basic Books, 1973.
35. Goleman, D. *The varieties of the meditative experience*. New York: Dutton, 1977.

36. Greenson, R. *The technique and practice of psychoanalysis.* New York: Int. Univ. Press, 1976.
37. Guénon, R. *Man and his becoming according to the vedanta.* London: Luzac, 1945.
38. Habermas, J. *Knowledge and human interests.* Boston: Beacon, 1971.
39. ———. *Legitimation crisis.* Boston: Beacon, 1975.
40. ———. *Theory and practice.* Boston: Beacon, 1973.
41. ———. *Communication and the evolution of society.* Boston: Beacon, 1976.
42. Hartmann, H. *Ego psychology and the problem of adaptation.* New York: Int. Univ. Press, 1958.
43. Hartshorne, C. *The logic of perfection.* La Salle: Open Court, 1973.
44. ———. *Whitehead's philosophy.* Lincoln: Univ. Nebr. Press, 1972.
45. Hegel, G. *The phenomenology of mind.* Ballie, J., trans. New York: Humanities Press, 1977.
46. ———. *Science of logic.* Johnston and Struthers, 2 vols., London: Allen & Unwin, 1951.
47. Horkheimer, M. *Critical theory.* New York: Seabury, 1972.
48. Hume, R., trans. *The 13 principal upanishads.* London: Oxford Univ. Press, 1974.
49. Ihde, D. *Hermeneutic phenomenology: The philosophy of Paul Ricoeur.* Evanston: Northwestern, 1971.
50. Jacobson, E. *The self and the object world.* New York: Int. Univ. Press, 1964.
51. James, W. *Varieties of religious experience.* New York: Collier, 1961.
52. Jonas, H. *The gnostic religion.* Boston: Beacon, 1963.
53. Jung, C. G. *The basic writings of* ———. DeLaszlo (ed.). New York: Modern Library, 1959.
54. Kohlberg, L., and Gilligan, C. "The adolescent as philosopher." In Harrison, S., and McDermott, J. (eds.), *New Directions in Childhood Psychopathology.* New York: Int. Univ. Press, 1980.
55. Kaplan, P. "An excursion into the 'undiscovered country.' " In Garfield, C. (ed.), *Rediscovery of the Body.* New York: Dell, 1977.
56. Lasch, C. *The culture of narcissism.* New York: Norton, 1979.

57. Loevinger, J. *Ego development*. San Francisco: Jossey-Bass, 1976.
58. Maliszwewski, M., *et al.* "A phenomenological typology of intensive meditation." *ReVision,* vol. 4, no. 2, 1981.
59. Marin, P. "The new narcissism." *Harpers*, Oct. 1975.
60. Marx, K. *Selected writings*. Bottomore, T. (ed.). London, 1956.
61. Maslow, A. *The farther reaches of human nature*. New York: Viking, 1971.
62. Merton, R. *Social theory and social structure*. Glencoe: Free Press, 1957.
63. Mishra, R. *Yoga sutras*. Garden City, New York: Anchor, 1973.
64. Needham, J. *Science and civilization in China*. vol. 2, London: Cambridge, 1956.
65. Needleman, J. *Lost Christianity*. New York: Doubleday, 1980.
66. Neumann, E. *The origins and history of consciousness*. Princeton: Princeton Univ. Press, 1973.
67. Ogilvy, J. *Many dimensional man*. New York: Oxford Univ. Press, 1977.
68. Palmer, R. *Hermeneutics*. Evanston, 1969.
69. Parsons, T. *The social system*. Glencoe, 1951.
70. Piaget, J. *The essential*——. Gruber, H., and Voneche, J. (eds.). New York: Basic Books, 1977.
71. Polanyi, M. *Personal knowledge*. Chicago: Univ. of Chic. Press, 1958.
72. Radin, P. *The world of primitive man*. New York: Grove, 1960.
73. Rank, O. *Psychology and the soul*. New York: Perpetua, 1961.
74. Rank, O. *Beyond psychology*. New York: Dover, 1958.
75. Rapaport, D. *Organization and pathology of thought*. New York: Columbia, 1951.
76. Rapaport, D. and Gill, M. "The points of views and assumptions of metapsychology." *Int. J. Psychoanal.,* vol. 40, 1959.
77. Robbins, T., and Anthony, D. "New religious movements and the social system." *Ann. Rev. Soc. Sc. Rel.* 2, 1978.
78. ——. *In gods we trust*. San Francisco: Transaction Books, 1981.
79. Ricoeur, P. *Freud and philosophy*. New Haven: Yale, 1970.

80. Roheim, G. *Magic and schizophrenia.* New York, I.U.P. 1955.
81. Schuon, F. *Logic and transcendence.* New York: Harper, 1975.
82. Schutz, A. *The phenomenology of the social world.* Evanston: Northwestern, 1967.
83. Schutz, A. and Luckmann, T. *The structures of the life-world.* Evanston: Northwestern, 1973.
84. Selman, R. "The relation of role-taking to the development of moral judgement in children." *Child Development,* 42, 1971.
85. Singh, K. *Surat shabd yoga.* Berkeley: Images Press, 1975.
86. Smith, H. *Forgotten truth.* New York: Harper, 1976.
87. Sullivan, H. *The interpersonal theory of psychiatry.* New York: Norton, 1953.
88. Suzuki, D. T. *Studies in the lankavatara sutra.* London: Routledge and Kegan Paul, 1968.
89. Taimni, I. *The science of yoga.* Wheaton: Quest, 1975.
90. Takakusu, J. *The essentials of Buddhist philosophy.* Honolulu: Univ. of Hawaii, 1956.
91. Teilhard de Chardin, P. *The future of man.* New York: Harper, 1964.
92. Twemlow, S., et al. "The out-of-body experience." Submitted *Am. J. Psych.*
93. Washburn, M. "The bimodal and tri-phasic structures of human experience." *ReVision,* vol. 3, no. 2, 1980.
94. Watts, A. *Beyond theology.* Cleveland: Meridian, 1975.
95. Werner, H. *Comparative psychology of mental development.* New York: Int. Univ. Press, 1957.
96. ———. "The concept of development from a comparative and organismic point of view." In Harris (ed.), *The concept of development.* Minneapolis: Univ. of Minnesota, 1957.
97. Whitehead, A. *Process and reality.* New York: Free Press, 1969.
98. Whyte, L. L. *The next development in man.* New York: Mentor, 1950.
99. Wilber, K. "Eye to eye." *ReVision,* vol. 2, no. 1, 1979.
100. ———. "Physics, mysticism, and the new holographic paradigm." *ReVision,* vol. 2, no. 2, 1979.
101. ———. *The Atman project.* Wheaton: Quest, 1980.
102. ———. "The pre/trans fallacy." *ReVision,* vol. 3, no. 2, 1980.

103. ———. "Ontogenetic development—two fundamental patterns." *Journal of Transpersonal Psychology,* vol. 13, no. 1, 1981.
104. ———. "Reflections on the new age paradigm." *Re-Vision,* vol. 4, no. 1, 1981.
105. ———. *Up from Eden.* New York: Anchor/Doubleday, 1981.
106. ———. "Legitimacy, authenticity, and authority in the new religions." Privately circulated ms.
107. Wilden, A. "Libido as language." *Psychology Today.* May 1972.
108. Zilboorg, G. "Fear of death." *Psychoanal. Quat.* vol. 12, 1943.

Recommended Reading: An Introduction to Transpersonal Psychology

109. Assagioli, R. *Psychosynthesis.* New York: Viking, 1965.
110. Benoit, H. *The supreme doctrine.* New York: Viking, 1959.
111. Campbell, J. *The masks of God.* 4 vols. New York: Viking, 1959–1968.
112. Fadiman, J., and Frager, R. *Personality and personal growth.* New York: Harper, 1976.
113. Goleman, D. *The varieties of the meditative experience.* New York: Dutton, 1977.
114. Govinda, L. *Foundations of Tibetan mysticism.* New York: Weiser, 1969.
115. Green, E., and Green, A. *Beyond biofeedback.* New York: Delacorte, 1977.
116. Grof, S. *Realms of the human unconscious.* New York: Viking, 1975.
117. Hixon, L. *Coming home.* New York: Anchor, 1978.
118. Huxley, A. *The perennial philosophy.* New York: Harper, 1944.
119. James, W. *The varieties of religious experience.* New York: Collier, 1961.
120. Jung, C. G. *Memories, dreams, and reflections.* New York: Vintage, 1965.
121. Kornfield, J. *Living Buddhist masters.* Santa Cruz: Unity, 1977.
122. LeShan, L. *Alternate Realities.* New York: Ballantine, 1977.

123. Maslow, A. *The farther reaches of human nature.* New York: Viking, 1977.
124. Needleman, J. *Lost Christianity.* New York: Doubleday, 1980.
125. Neumann, E. *The origins and history of consciousness.* Princeton: Princeton Univ. Press, 1973.
126. Roberts, T. (ed.). *Four psychologies applied to education.* Cambridge: Schenkman, 1974.
127. Schumacher, E. *A guide for the perplexed.* New York: Harper, 1977.
128. Smith, H. *Forgotten truth.* New York: Harper, 1976.
129. Tart, C. *States of consciousness.* New York: Dutton, 1975.
130. Walsh, R., and Vaughan, F. *Beyond ego.* Los Angeles: Tarcher, 1980.
131. White, J. *The highest state of consciousness.* New York: Doubleday, 1973.
132. Wilber, K. *The Atman project.* Wheaton: Quest, 1980.
133. ———. *Up from Eden.* New York: Anchor/Doubleday, 1981.
134. Woods, R. (ed.). *Understanding mysticism.* New York: Image, 1981.

INDEX

A

Active independence, 100–102
Actively passive surrender, 100, 102–105
Adaptation, structural, 76, 126, 128
  defined, 72–74
  in exoteric religion, 58
Adolescence, 100–105
Ajna chakra, 29, 30
Alayavijnana, 30
Al-Hallaj, 63, 91
American civil religion, 63, 81–82, 92, 106–109
Anandamayakosa, 25, 30
Angst, 50–51
Annamayakosa, 19, 25
Anthony, Dick, 84–90, 94, 106, 108, 109–110
Anti-laws, 95–97, 127
Apprehension, 133–134
Aquinas, Saint Thomas, 60
Archaic level, 19n, 130
Arieti, S., 20, 22
Aristotle, 3, 60
Astrology, 96
Atman Project, The (Wilber), x, 26, 125
Augustine, Saint, 3
Aurobindo, viii, 24, 27, 28, 30, 31, 58

B

Baldwin, J., 16
Becker, Ernest, 49, 51, 52, 57
Belief, 69, 73, 93
  defined, 65–67
  in exoteric religion, 58, 67
Bell, D., 78
Bellah, Robert, 4, 14, 23, 80–87, 92, 97, 106–108
Berdyaev, Nikolai Aleksandrovich, 24
Berger, Peter, 4, 73n, 129
Bergson, Henri, viii
Bioenergy, 19
Biofeedback, 100
"Blue pearl," 29
Body level, 35, 36, 39, 86, 104, 112, 117

C

Neolithic era, 22
Newton, Sir Isaac, 60, 76
Nietzsche, Friedrich Wilhelm, viii, 76
Nirodh, 30
Nirvikalpa samadhi, 30, 32, 44
Norms, 77

O

Occult, 96
Oedipal mythology, 8, 93
Ogilvy, J., 78
Oppression, 40–41, 42, 115
Out-laws, 95

P

Padmasambhava, 63
Paleolithic era, 22, 52, 62, 76
Panenhenic mysticism, 32–33, 70–71,
    87
Papal encyclicals, 60
Paradoxical reason, 113, 117, 133
Parsons, Talcott, 1, 4, 9, 108
Passive dependence, 100–105
Patanjali, 3, 44
Paul, Saint, 44, 69
Peak experience, ix, 58, 61, 72–74
    defined, 68–71
Perennial philosophy, 1, 3–5, 86
Perspectivism, 77–79
Phenomenological-hermeneutics (see
    Hermeneutics)
"Phenomenological-Structuralist
    Approach to the Scientific Study
    of Religion, A" (Anthony),
    89–91
Phenomenology, 13
Philosophia perennis, 1, 3–5, 86
Physical level, 19, 25, 37–38, 39, 41,
    42, 44, 47, 112, 116
Piaget, Jean, 8, 16, 19, 20, 39, 47,
    53, 73, 77, 90
Plato, 3, 4
Plotinus, 3
"Polar development," 21
"Political Aspects of the Quietistic
    Revival" (Wuthnow), 107
Positivists, 55–56
Practical interest, 112
Prana, 19, 25, 36, 44

155

S

Translation (*cont.*):
  mis-, 130–131, 132
Trans-laws, 98–99, 107, 128
"Transpersonal," 3
Transpersonal psychology, viii–ix, 3,
  7, 108–109, 126
Trans-rationality, 30, 61, 69, 80, 92,
  94, 123–124
Tremlow, S., 126
Turiya, 25, 31

U

Ultimate level (*see* Causal level)
United States:
  Civil religion of, 63, 81–82, 92,
    106–109
  new religions in, 91–109, 126
Upanishads, 32
Up from Eden (Wilber), vii, x, 24,
  35, 52

V

Vajrayana, 27, 63, 109
Varieties of Religious Experience
  (James), 14, 72
Vedanta, 19, 20, 25–26, 30, 32, 33,
  60, 63, 88
Vedas, 32
Vertical emancipatory interest,
  117–118, 132
Vico, Giovanni Battista, 4
Vijnanamayakosa, 25, 28, 30
Vision logic, 27–29, 44
Voodoo, 96

W

Walsh, Roger, xiii
Watts, Alan W., 33
Weber, Max, 4, 23, 75, 107
Werner, H., 16, 39, 47, 77, 78
Whitehead, Alfred North, 36
Whyte, L. L., 52
Wilber, Ken:
  methodology of, 121–135
  works by, vii, x, 24, 47, 105, 125
  as Zen Buddhist, 25–26
Witches, 127
Wordsworth, William, 32
Worldview, 76–77
Wuthnow, Robert, 107